JOSEPH GAVI

JOSEPH GAVI

Young Hero of the Minsk Ghetto

CARLTON JACKSON

Acclaim Press
MORLEY, MISSOURI

Acclaim Press
— Your Next Great Book —
P.O. Box 238
Morley, MO 63767
(573) 472-9800
www.acclaimpress.com

Design by:

Steward&Wise
GRAPHIC DESIGN

Designer: Mary Ellen Sikes
Cover Design: Emily Sikes

Library of Congress Cataloging-in-Publication Data

Jackson, Carlton.
  Joseph Gavi--young hero of the Minsk ghetto / by Carlton Jackson. -- Rev. ed.
     p. cm.
  Includes bibliographical references and index.
  ISBN-13: 978-1-935001-38-6 (alk. paper)
  ISBN-10: 1-935001-38-8 (alk. paper)
1. Gavi, Joseph. 2. Jews--Persecutions--Belarus--Minsk. 3. Jews--Belarus--Minsk--Biography. 4. Holocaust, Jewish (1939-1945)--Belarus--Minsk--Personal narratives. 5. World War, 1939-1945--Jewish resistance--Belarus--Minsk. 6. Minsk (Belarus)--Biography. I. Title.
  DS135.B382M565 2010
  940.53'18092--dc22
  [B]
                                2009053979

Printed in the United States of America
First Printing: 2010
10 9 8 7 6 5 4 3 2 1

Additional copies may be purchased from Acclaim Press.

CONTENTS

Preface 7

Foreword 17

Chapter One – The Raised Fist 25

Chapter Two – The Holocaust Strikes Home..................... 42

Chapter Three – The Partisans.............................. 53

Chapter Four – Home to Minsk 82

Chapter Five – The Mountains............................. 97

Chapter Six – Coping with the Systems............... 125

Chapter Seven – Thinking American 164

Chapter Eight – Becoming American................... 177

A Note on Sources... 196

Index... 198

PREFACE

JOSEPH GAVI:
"AN UNFORGETTABLE BRIGHTNESS"

One of the many sources of pleasure that I have received since *Joseph Gavi: Young Hero of the Minsk Ghetto* was first published in 2000 is being involved in signings at bookstores and book fairs that Joseph and I attended throughout Kentucky, Tennessee, and Illinois. To be sure, and rightly so, would-be book buyers came out to see Joseph— he was the attraction—the "noun"—and I was the "verb." And, as we all know, nouns are more interesting and appealing than verbs. And, of course, you have to have a noun before you can have a verb.

We, Joseph and I, had wonderful times at these gatherings, and Joseph regaled his audiences with one wondrous story after another. Primarily he talked about how much he "felt at home" in the United States, particularly in Louisville, Kentucky, where he and his family settled permanently after their journey to America in 1978. Occasionally, however, he would embark upon stories from his childhood and what life had been like in the Old Country.

At the book fair in Frankfort, Kentucky, for example, in November 2001, he talked about the "Commissar of Ze Sheets," in the part of Minsk where he was born, and lived through his early childhood. Well, the people around him (including me, and my friend and fellow author, Lowell Harrison, who shared our table) kept wondering what he meant. Just exactly what was a "Commissar of Ze Sheets?" Pressed for details, he explained. There was a functionary in each ward of every political department in the country who had the job of visiting all the out-houses in the area, to check the inside—and even down the hole, for that matter—to see if anyone had used a newspaper with Josef Stalin's photo on it. If he found any "incriminating" evidence, the householder would be dragged before the local Communist Committee, and made to answer for his "crimes against the state." Thus, he was the "Commissar of Ze Sheets;" whether that word referred to a newspaper sheet or something else, Joseph never really said, but the story certainly gave us some hilarious moments.

The organizers of the fair put helium-filled balloons at various spaces throughout the big arena at Kentucky State College. At the end of the day, both Joseph and I took pleasure in bursting each one of them (mostly with ball-point pens) over our table, to our delight and perplexed looks from many of the other participants at the fair. What the hell? It was the end of a long hard but thoroughly enjoyable day and we figured that a bit of silly revelry wouldn't hurt anybody. Come to think of it, the world could use a bit more of this. Fortunately, everybody at the fair saw the fun of it, and laughed with us, and some even began popping their own balloons. "I've been wanting to do this all day," Joseph gleefully remarked.

Joseph and I went to so many places that it would be difficult to recall all of them in a short Preface. An audience of over a hundred showed up at Barnes & Noble in Bowling Green, Kentucky, where Joseph spoke and we sold out all the copies of the book we had with us. Even the publisher, Douglas Sikes, didn't have enough copies on that particular occasion. We went to several bookstores in Louisville, a city Joseph loved and where he was well known. A man walked by our table wearing a brightly colored Hawaiian shirt. "Nice shirt," I called out. He said, "Thank you," and kept on walking. I yelled to him, "Hey, if I can brag on your shirt, you can at least look at our book." He backed up, and wound up buying a copy. After that, Joseph was convinced that I was a "master salesman." I am not; it is just that we had a wonderful product to offer to the public. But for the man in the "Hawaiian shirt, thank you, and Aloha!"

Joseph came to Western Kentucky University, where I was a professor of history, to speak to the local chapter of the History Honor Society,

Phi Alpha Theta. It was an overflow audience, as Joseph recounted his experiences in the Minsk ghetto. (One insensitive guest remarked afterwards that the Holocaust was not exactly the "right kind" of "after dinner" speech). On this occasion, Joseph Gavi was presented with a certificate signed by Governor Paul Patton, making Joseph a Kentucky Colonel. His framed "colonelcy" still has pride of place on one of the shelves in Gavi's Restaurant in Louisville.

I remember one harrowing trip I made with Colonel Gavi. A bookstore in Skokie, Illinois, just outside Chicago, arranged for the two of us to come up there for a signing. Joseph drove, and all I can say is that he was a better restaurateur than driver. All the way toward Chicago, I kept thinking about the stories Joseph had told me dealing with how he learned to drive in the first place; how he pushed the accelerator one day instead of the brake and ran headlong into a funeral truck, spilling the corpse out onto the pavement. On Interstate 65 Joseph did not once get out of the left lane in his little Honda, all the while keeping up a steady conversation with me—despite my continued admonitions to keep his eye on the road—about the miseries of the Old Soviet Union and the glories of the United States. He passed everything in sight; the only positive thing I could say about the trip is that we arrived early. Joseph was a wonderful man, but I decided that if there were any more long trips in the future, I would do the driving. The next morning, when we were to come back to Louisville, God help us, the Chicago area was going through one of its famous (or infamous?) series of thunderstorms. The rain, wind, and thunder and fierce lightning, however, slowed Joe down, for which I was profoundly grateful. Joseph told me one time that he loved this country (the USA) so much that he was "in a hurry" to explain it to as many people as would listen to him. Maybe that's why he had such a "lead-foot" when he got behind the wheel of a car.

Further accentuating this "speedy" point was when his first grandson, David, turned 16, and wanted a driver's license. Joseph picked up David from school and drove him to LaGrange. Unfortunately, his birth certificate was written entirely in Italian (David's birth in Italy is recounted in Chapter Eight of the first edition), and the driving instructor insisted on a translation. David went on: "They stopped testing at 4 and it was already 3:30; where were we going to find an Italian translator? I remembered my Spanish teacher saying that he knew a little Italian. I told my grandfather this. The next words out of his mouth [were]"don't you ever drive the

9

way I'm about to." They made the 15 minute trip back to Crestwood in 7 minutes, found the teacher, who took only 5 minutes to do the necessary translations and then got back to LaGrange in 6 minutes. "He ran a red light or two," David wistfully recalls. "I got my license that day."[1]

Joseph spoke at many school gatherings, both elementary and high school, in the Louisville area. He relished these invitations because he wanted to tell young people about the horrors of World War II and the miseries that ghetto life entailed. "I have an obligation to tell these stories," he asserted. We must never quit talking about what the Nazis did to Europe and the world in the late 1930s and on well into the 1940s. "Telling the story of the Holocaust," Joseph claimed, "was important because it could happen again. Look at Bosnia, Rwanda, Kosovo."[2] And, of course, since this statement, consider what has happened to the Darfur region of the Sudan.

Not long ago I heard a person remark that there "have been enough books on the Holocaust. We need to get past it." My response was "No, No, No. There haven't been nearly *enough* books on the Holocaust. We need to keep this miserable horror before the eyes of the civilized world, hopefully to prevent another Holocaust or its "cleaned up" version, "ethnic cleansing," from ever happening again. We live in a time when morons and bigots either say that the Holocaust never happened, or if it did, it wasn't all that much of a big deal.[3] The evidence is more than amply clear; Adolph Hitler was intent on a "Final Solution." It is documented beyond reproach that over six million Jews lost their lives to the Holocaust in World War II, simply because they were Jews, and we in the modern world of the 21st Century must never forget that statistic. We are bound by this obligation.

As Joseph's grandson, Gabriel (Gaba) put it, the Holocaust requires "constant re-entry" into our minds. We must "recognize the mistakes we... make, so that we do not follow them again."[4]

I read recently that the Holocaust is a subject that perhaps should not be discussed "except among ourselves,"[5] that is, only the Jews who personally suffered at the hands of Nazi thugs, or their descendants. "No, No, No," was my response to *this* assertion. The Holocaust—its ramifications for the

[1]David Gavi, Email to the author, 29 April 2008.

[2]Steve Chaplin, "Students Get History of WWII from Man Who Helped Make it," *The Courier-Journal* (Louisville, KY). April 16, 2000.

[3]See David Margolick's review of Tova Reich, *My Holocaust* (New York: HarperCollins Publishers), in The *New York Times* Book Review, May 27, 2007.

[4]Email, Gabriel Gavi to the author; 29 January 2008.

[5]Margolick's review of Tova Reich, *My Holocaust.*"

present, its meaning, and its history—belongs to all humankind, who must see to it that such a horror does not occur again.

Joseph and I actually did have more in common with each other than either of us in our early youth realized. I fought "wars" at Bagley Elementary School in Alabama, where we always defeated the Nazis or "Noksis," as we called them. We always won. But that was not the case with one of our unknown compatriots at the time: Joseph Gavi. He fought these wars in a starkly realistic manner; our lives were in the realms of Imagination; his was on the Line. And there was a huge difference between the two.

What else can I say about Joseph Gavi that I have not already said? I wish to add that my family and Joseph's family became good and close friends. We visited each other in our homes whenever there was an opportunity. Our second son, Matthew, stands six feet four inches tall. He has a Master's Science Degree that resonated well with Dr. Joseph Gavi's PhD in Science. They talked about things that I did not understand, but they were both on the same track, and all I could do was just listen to them in confusion and admiration as they talked about various scientific subjects. I can assure you, seeing Matthew at 6 feet 4, and Joseph Gavi at 4 feet 11, was a sight; something else altogether. Joseph came up about to Matthew's waist, but the respect and camaraderie that the two demonstrated for each other was manifest.

One of the great honors that came to Joseph because of this book (and by extension, to me, because I had written it) was when, in February 2002, Joseph was publicly acknowledged by the Senate of the Kentucky General Assembly. The commendation was sponsored by Senator Brett Guthrie of Bowling Green. Both Joseph and I stood proudly before the Senate as the Clerk read off a three-page, single-spaced explanation—which included his youth, ghetto experiences, and activities in the Naleboke Forest which saved many families and friends from the Germans, of why Joseph Gavi should be honored, and why this was such a fitting tribute to one of the most loyal and patriotic citizens the United States and Kentucky could ever hope to find. At the end of the reading, all the Senators and spectators gave Joseph a well-deserved standing ovation. And, I have to say, more than one person in the audience teared up. Considerably. Including myself.

"And what does Joseph's own family think of his legacy? Why should Joseph's memory be kept alive," I have asked.

His son, Alex, recounted that both his father and mother were East Europeans who witnessed the atrocities of World War II, both of them "missing their childhoods."[6] Alex's maternal grandmother, Sima (mentioned in the text) "had to drink from the puddles where camels just urinated moments before." Resilience of the "human spirit" made Sima, her daughter, Ida, and Ida's husband, Joseph Gavi, "triumphant" in the Human Spirit.[7]

One of Joseph's grandsons, Gabriel (Gaba) said that Joseph Gavi had seen perils and evils; yet had maintained "honor, dignity, and integrity."[8] Even with Joseph's short stature, 4' 11", Gaba felt that he was standing on the shoulders of Giants: "I could go over any mountain."[9]

One of the fondest memories Gaba has of his grandfather was Joseph's passion about politics. "He loved this country [the United States] with all his heart." He compared Joseph to the horse, Secretariat, who, like Joseph, had an irregularly sized heart. Joseph would frequently wave his finger at customers (even jeopardizing his business with them if he had to), some of whom "were twice his size," preaching the "truth" about patriotism, politics and life. "It is something he was never shy about," reports Gaba, "and something to which he never budged. He might have been a stubborn man, but it was always with conviction, and with the greater good in mind."[10]

One of his son Alex's favorite memories conjured up shoe polish. This reminiscence pertained to the slathers of polish Joseph always put on his mountaineering boots before ascending a mountain. But the hours and even days before the mountain climbing remain impressed in Alex's mind. He, with his parents and older brother, Isaac, spent several days in a private train car going from Minsk to the mountain regions. With the Caucasus in the distance, they spent a happy ten hour bus ride, where, at the end, the "crystal mountain air exhilarated and inebriated one's whole being...." "My dad made it all possible for the four of us." Even though Joseph's own way—but not his family's—to the mountains was paid by the government, money was tight. "We were poor," Alex modestly proclaims. However, Alex avows, "What my parents had given me could never be replaced by any amount of money in the world." Not surprisingly, the Gavi family was close, and it stayed that way in the USSR, Chicago, and Louisville, Kentucky. In fact, to Joseph, *everything* was family. An admirer said of him: "From the time of the Minsk ghetto he [Joseph] had a strong feeling for

[6]Email, Alex Gavi to the author; 30 January 2008.
[7]Ibid.
[8]Email, Gabriel Gavi to the author, 29 January 2008.
[9]Ibid.
[10]Ibid.

the idea of FAMILY. He understood at that young age that saving others was imperative to the value of his own existence."[11]

Joseph may have been one of Louisville's best-known restaurateurs, but he was also known in another capacity. Very frequently, especially since the end of the Cold War, many foreigners came to these shores from the Balkan countries as well as those in the old Soviet Union. Court cases, both civil and criminal, inevitably occurred between and among these new arrivals and language became a problem as English-speaking lawyers and judges tried to settle things. Joseph (and Ida as well) were frequently summoned to act as interpreters in northern Kentucky and southern Indiana court cases. The legal communities, composed primarily of lawyers and judges, knew who Joseph Gavi was, and honored and respected him—and ate at his restaurant.

And so did a lot of policemen who worked just across from Gavi's Restaurant on Seventh Street, the biggest police station in Louisville. Every day, Louisville's finest sprinted across the thoroughfare to have scrambled eggs, cheeseburgers, or (on Thursdays) beef stroganoff. Ironically, even though it was directly across the street from the big police station, Gavi's Restaurant was routinely burglarized during the 1990s and early 2000s. Joseph, however, did not blame his friends in the police department for this unfortunate situation. He just kept on telling them about the glories of American democracy.

He was not jingoistic in this endeavor. One should not ascribe any kind of "Right Wing, hard-core evangelistic" connotations to his message about the greatness of America. It had nothing to do with religion; on the contrary, it was a matter of comparison. Most of his remarks about either the Soviet Union (or Belarus for that matter) or America came down to the differences he saw between the two of them. In reference to civil rights, privacy, dignity, self-respect, prosperity, personal advancement, there was no contest: It was America all the way. *The telling of that story* was Joseph Gavi's great legacy to his adopted country, the United States, and by extension, to the world. This was his "Unforgettable Brightness."[12]

In late 2000 the family Gavi of Louisville decided to spend the Christmas vacation with Ida's extended family in Miami, Florida. While in this southern city, on January 1, 2001, Joseph suffered a near-fatal heart attack. Instead of returning to Louisville when the holidays ended, he lingered on for weeks in a Miami hospital. Finally, back in Louisville, he ultimately

[11]Juliet Baasch, Email to the author; 9 July 2008.
[12]Email, Alex Gavi to the author, 21 January 2008.

started back to work in the family restaurant. The only noticeable change about Joseph after his ordeal was that he had grown a beard. He was taking so many blood-thinning agents that he was afraid that a nick from shaving could turn out badly. I teased him about the beard, telling him that he looked like a prophet out of the Old Testament, a statement that amused him.

He continued to work, to give speeches to Louisville area high schools, translate for the court systems and, seemingly, in just about every important way resumed his previous life-style. One day in late 2002, however, driving from the restaurant to his home in Crestwood, he suffered another seizure, and this time were the complications of injuries from the car crash. On December 5, 2002, he passed away in a Louisville hospital. His big, over-sized heart just gave out on him.

Reporter, Paula Burba, recounted Joseph's life in the obituary she wrote for the Louisville *Courier-Journal*. She emphasized Joseph's fondness for relating his experiences to various audiences, especially to elementary and high school students. "Never wait to tell your story," he told a Holocaust Remembrance Day observance. "As soon as we forget, it's possible to happen again."[13] Louisville mayor, Dave Armstrong, a long-time friend of Joseph's, and frequent diner at the "Courthouse," (a name many policemen, court personnel, judges, and other government employees, as well as jurors and lawyers, called the restaurant) said Joseph "was proud to be an American. Nearly every time I saw him, he would bring up something about human rights.... "[14]

There were, of course, numerous tributes and memorials to the life of Joseph Gavi. None was more touching than those from some of his own grandchildren. Gabriel (Gaba) wrote, just after Joseph's death, that when he thinks of his "burdens in life," Joseph always comes to mind. "...[A]t the age of ten he [Joseph] carried the weight of the world" on his shoulders. "Saving lives, fighting a war, escaping secretly in the night, and this is only the beginning."[15] "It's rare," he asserted, when you find that perfect rose, but it happens."

Another grandchild, Natalie Gavi (Alex's daughter) touchingly remembered her grandfather as a hero, always walking around with a smile, "giving a life supply of advice."[16] Joseph Gavi, said his loving granddaugh-

[13]Paula Burba, "Restaurateur Gavi Dies at age 71," *The Courier-Journal*, December 7, 2002.
[14]Ibid.
[15]G.G. [Gabriel, "Gaba," Gavi], "Joseph Gavi,"12:41 a.m., December 8, 2002. Unpublished essay.
[16]Natalie Gavi, "My Hero," Unpublished essay, September 18, 2004.

ter, Natalie, "made such an impact on everyone's life, and just by living by his examples can make anyone who knew him a better person."[17]

Less than a month after Joseph's passing, Mayor Armstrong proclaimed on behalf of the people of Louisville and, indeed, the Commonwealth, a "Joseph Gavi" dedication. "In recognition of the distinguished service rendered in the public interest, I, David L. Armstrong, Mayor of Louisville do hereby declare Joseph Gavi as a Distinguished Citizen." the proclamation read. Addressing Joseph directly (though he was deceased), this "Expression of Gratitude" was tendered, the proclamation proceeded to say, "with the sincere appreciation of your fellow citizens."[18]

A great deal of publicity in Bowling Green, Kentucky, attended the first publication of *Joseph Gavi: Young Hero of the Minsk Ghetto*. The Bowling Green *Daily News* ran a front-page story about Joseph in one of its Sunday editions,[19] followed by an interview of Joseph by the local TV channel and dramatic footage of WWII battle scenes. Joseph was the attraction here: I get back to the fact that Joseph was the noun and I was the verb. This is where the Barnes & Noble tie-in comes again. As I said before, we ran out of books, always a pleasant occurrence to authors of books. All over the community of Bowling Green, Kentucky, Jewish groups had connected with Joseph; he had come to BG on more than one occasion, to address members of not only Orthodox but Messianic Jewish groups as well.

Bowling Green resident, Jim Johnson, sponsored a program at his home on March 1, 2003, entitled "Remembering Joseph Gavi." Lloyd and Sam Davis provided special music by Wolfgang Amadeus Mozart, while Johnson and others presented special remarks. Memories and Reflections were given by Johnson, Jonathan Sacks, and the author of this book. Among the many remarks on that occasion, Joseph's deeds between 1942 and 1944 were recounted as he led the residents of the Minsk ghetto to safety in the Naleboke Forest, and then participated in the resistance actions against the German tyranny.

It will have occurred to the reader several pages back that when Joseph Gavi died, I lost one of the best friends I've ever had or expect to have. As explained above, he was an inspiration not only to me, but to my entire family as well. I feel greatly blessed and highly honored to have been his life's chronicler.

---

[17]Ibid.

[18]David L. Armstrong, Mayoral Proclamation to Joseph Gavi, 31 December 2002.

[19]See *Daily News* (Bowling Green, Kentucky), May 27, 2000. See also the *Herald-Leader* (Lexington, KY), September 17, 2000; and *College Heights Herald* (Bowling Green, KY), September 14, 2000.

The restaurant that bears his name still operates on South Seventh Street, just off Jefferson Boulevard. Ida, Zina, and David primarily run the place. It is still lively, especially when the policemen from across the street come in, joined by the lawyers and judges who come in droves for lunch, particularly on Thursdays, when beef stroganoff, perhaps the most famous meal at Gavi's, is served. If they can't make it in person, there's still a take-out service, far different today from what it was at the beginning, when Joseph could speak very little English. One person at the police station told me that she was "always comforted" when she wanted personal food delivery, it was almost always Ida who answered the telephone.

It is not the same, though, without Joseph. Patrons got used to this diminutive man going from one table to another, asking how their food was, and then how they liked the principles of democratic government—many times starting spirited discussions. The place is not the same either without Sam Bird, who was the counter cook for so many years. He died not long after Joseph did, at 62. One can only hope that there are still many joyous days ahead for Gavi's Restaurant.

Here with the second edition, I have people to thank just as I did when the original book was published back in 2000. I know that it is not particularly fashionable in books to thank one's publisher, but I cannot let this edition go to press without expressing my sincere gratitude to publisher Douglas Sikes. At the first edition of this book, he worked for another publisher; nowadays, he is a part of an up and coming press in Missouri, Acclaim Press. He was willing to take a chance with me back in 2000 and it has worked out just fine; to Doug, thank you!

I wish also to thank the chair of the WKU history department, Robert Dietle, for his continued support of this volume as well as my other publishing endeavors.

My family has grown some in the eight years since this book was originally published.

We have some new grandchildren to mention: Liam, Rowan, Oliver, Henry; and little Gwennyn Mindora; and David Daniel and Finn. And to Elaine. And to Ling. And to Arthur. And first, foremost, and always: Pat.

Carlton Jackson
Butler County, Kentucky, 2010

FOREWORD

The first thing one notices about Joseph Gavi is his deeply-set, dark brown eyes that soften and glare depending on the subject he is discussing. If family, they are soft; if Nazis or Communists, anything but. Through his eyes he lets the listener know his likes and dislikes, and his loves and hatreds.

The second noticeable thing about Joseph Gavi is his dimunitive size. Throughout most of his adult life, he has stood at five feet exactly. Arthritic displacements, however, have reduced his stature nowadays to four feet, eleven inches. By no means, however, should one mistake Joe's size for anything short of virility and strength. He reminds one of the story former Philippine ambassador, Carlos Romulo, used to tell about himself. He was very short, and one day he attended a meeting with colleagues, all of whom were six-footers or more. Someone asked Romulo how he felt being in a room with so many tall people in it. He replied: "I feel like a dime among nickels."

Joe Gavi survived the holocaust in World War II, while rescuing over 200 people from the Minsk ghetto; and fought with the Russian partisans – having both experiences before he was even a teen-ager. By the time he reached fifteen, he was a hardened – and hard drinking – veteran of the Soviet navy, and a hero of World War II. In a starkly real way, Joseph Gavi missed his youth. He went straight from infancy into manhood.

Shortly after World War II, Joseph Gavi became involved in government sponsored mountain climbing activities in the Caucasus Mountains. Many Soviet soldiers had died in these mountains during the war from lack of experience, and the Soviet government wanted to assure that such would never happen again.

Joseph is also Dr. Gavi, holding a Ph.D degree from the Institute of Physiology, Academy of Science, in Belarus. He is a former instructor and researcher in science at Minsk Polytechnic Institute. So how is it then that today he runs a well-known restaurant in Louisville, Kentucky? That story is the subject of this book.

I became interested in Joseph Gavi when I read a short article in a newspaper in 1995 dealing with Memorial Day. A number of immigrants living in the Louisville area were mentioned, including Joe. The story gave only the briefest of outlines about Joe: the Minsk ghetto, the partisans, the navy – all before he was a teenager. The last sentence identified him as the proprietor and operator of Gavi's Restaurant, a popular luncheon place in Louisville (especially for baked chicken) for the police (the police station is just across the street), lawyers, and judges from the nearby Justice Center.

I called Information, and five minutes later I was talking with Joseph Gavi. Had anyone ever written his life story? No. Would he let me do it? Perhaps, but he would have to meet me first, of course.

From early summer 1995 to late summer 1997, I spent many Saturday afternoons in Joe's restaurant. I decided simply to let him talk: I could tie any loose threads together later. As he spoke, I had a tape recorder running, and I also typed his words on my little laptop computer. He spoke slowly and distinctly, and spelled out words for me as we went along for, undeniably, his English is better than my Russian. As his notes accumulated, I began to write the narrative. Each time I finished fifteen to twenty pages, I sent them to Joe, and he added to and deleted from, the developing manuscript. Then, I sent the entire manuscript to Joe, and he went through the same process again. I believe that by using this method, we have eliminated many errors of fact and interpretation. I am, of course, wholly responsible for any errors that remain.

I used some secondary sources, especially with ghetto conditions in Minsk and the partisans in the nearby woods. I wanted to be sure I was depicting everything as correctly as I possibly could. Likewise with the immigration processes out of the Soviet Union during the mid to late 1970s. Interestingly enough, I could find no secondary materials on the Soviet mountain climbing programs just after World War II. Other than these few secondary sources, the information for this book has come over-whelmingly from the recollections of one man: Joseph Gavi, and to a lesser extent, his wife, Ida.

I am aiming this book at a general reading audience, one who appreci-ates not only what we have here in America, but as well is concerned with other, less fortunate, populations of the world. There is a time for compas-sion, and I hope this book speaks to that point.

In this book, I speak with two voices: my own and Joseph Gavi's. I try to place Joseph's life into an historical context as the manuscript progresses, to show to the extent necessary those historical events that had an impact on his and his fellow citizens' lives.

On personal matters, as far as possible, I will let Joseph himself speak directly to the reader. Sometimes in the interviews Joseph got so excited with what he was telling me that he switched to the present tense, just as though the event were happening right then and there. I have tried to incorporate these special moments into the manuscript, and I hope I have struck a balance between dialogue and documentary. This approach hopefully will capture both the historical and memoir characteristics I wish to create in this book.

In no way is this work "regional." Joseph Gavi might live in Louisville, Kentucky, but his story is universal. This book deals with the horrors of war, unsettled times that usually follow, and the inhumanity that mankind is capable of inflicting on itself. Most importantly, it is also about the uplifting of the human spirit; the basic drive of human beings to survive. Not just survive, as in Joseph Gavi's case, but to triumph after finally realizing that his "comradeship" in the USSR could not last, but that his "citizenship" in the USA could.

Chapter One deals with the German invasion of Russia, and the creation of the Minsk ghetto. At first many of the Minsk Jews, especially the older ones, thought the Germans would be better than their Communist bosses. They quickly found out their mistake.

Chapter Two describes the German "aktions" against the Minsk Jews, and the pogroms against them in which some Byelorussians participated. Joseph lost many members of his family in these continuing atrocities.

Chapter Three shows Joseph slipping out of the ghetto, using his shortness of stature to elude the ever-present German guards, and joining the Russian partisans. Though he was highly useful to the partisans, neither he nor they particularly liked each other. It was their common hatred of Germans that helped them get along.

"Home To Minsk," Chapter Four, shows Joseph going into Poland as the war ended, and then being re-united with his mother and little brother. He tried to get into a military school, but wound up in the Soviet navy instead, when he was all of twelve years old. By the time he was a teen-ager, he was a seasoned veteran of both the Soviet army and the Soviet navy.

Chapter Five, "The Mountains," depicts a relatively happy time in Joseph Gavi's life in the Soviet Union. In the mountains, he frequently asserted, one can be a real human being.

In Chapter Six, however, "Coping With the Systems," though he has been around it all his life, it seems only now, when he has become an adult, that he recognizes the fierce bureaucracy with which Soviet citizens have to contend. He has always known, too, that the Soviet system is greatly anti-Semitic, and it now begins to trouble him greatly. In fact, he is fired from his job as an academic, simply because he is a Jew.

"Thinking American," Chapter Seven, shows Joe's fairly slow but steady realization that he will have to leave his homeland and go elsewhere if his life is to be fulfilling. He is loyal to his country, but he painfully finds that his country is not loyal to him. The trials and tribulations of getting an exit visa from the Soviet Union are tabulated in this chapter.

The last chapter is "Becoming American," in which Joseph and his family marvel at the wonders of the New World. One very simple matter, overlooked by most Americans, but very important to many other people around the world is that in the United States you can buy food for longer periods than just one day. And it took a while for Joseph to become familiar with the intricacies of the checking system. Rather quickly, in fact, Joseph Gavi changed from "comrade" to "citizen," and became a Capitalist, in the finest sense of that word.

As always, I have people to thank in helping me to prepare this manuscript. My first thanks, of course, go to Joseph and his wife, Ida Gavi. They were unstinting and enthusiastic as they told me their stories. Not the least of my gratitude in this respect is the friendship that has developed between Joseph and myself. We come from essentially the same generation, but the lives we led were indeed worlds apart, except that we both did – somewhat surprisingly in each case – become academics. I feel highly honored and privileged to have become a part of Joseph Gavi's life. And I do not have the words to express my pleasure at being his life's chronicler.

I thank Professor Lowell H. Harrison for reading the entire manuscript, and giving valuable advice. WKU Professor Hugh Phillips provided some much needed translations, for which I am grateful.

My family, as in the past, encouraged my efforts: Beverly, Hilary, Daniel, and Matthew; and Colleen, Megan, and Katharine; and Travis, Patrick, and Austin; and Grace, and Steve. And, as always, Pat. Thank you very much, indeed.

Carlton Jackson,
Western Kentucky University

JOSEPH GAVI

Young Hero of the Minsk Ghetto

CHAPTER ONE

THE RAISED FIST

I am Joseph Gavi and I am nine years old.

My dream is always the same:

The big tree on my street I have seen always, even since I was born. One day I walk by and it is gone – cut, and the only thing left is a big, ugly stump. I am puzzled; what does this mean, my tree being cut down? I have always seen it on my street and have come to expect it on my walks. It is my tree!

Beyond the surprise and anger at seeing my tree missing, is the long line of people – many of whom I know. There is my cousin, Fera, standing right there in front of the stump.

But even more sinister to me, there is this huge guy with an ax. He stands expectantly, waiting for his next "customer." His ax blade is bloody already from his day's work, and it is still even the morning.

Despite the axman's presence, the people in the line are at ease with one another, friendly, talking about their plans for this day. They constantly crane their heads to see what is up ahead of them – just around a slight curve – they cannot see the end of the queue. Nothing much, if anything, is happening, they conclude, so they go back to their usual discussions of everyday life in Minsk, the capital of Soviet Byelorussia.[1] Just why they are standing in the line does not even come

---

[1] Today, the late 1990s, Minsk is the capital of the independent state of Belarus.

up. Perhaps it is because long queues are such a part of their lives.

But when they turn the curve, everything changes. They see the axman crouching with his bloody tool, and the crowd stirs, only to be stopped and put back in place by armed soldiers.

I look behind me and cannot see the end of the line; I look in front and I see the person who is next to the stump of my favorite tree bending over and putting his bare neck on it. The axman straightens up, raises his ax, and with a heavy heft, brings the ax down onto the top of the person's neck, severing it from his body with one clean, powerful blow.

I am terrified at this scene. I do not scream. I do not believe I can scream. I look back at those still in the line. There is my entire family: Mama, Papa, both sets of grandparents, aunts, uncles, cousins – the whole group – are waiting their turn for the axman. I see them come closer and closer to the stump. I watch with mute terror as my loved ones somehow get in front of me and go before the axman. Finally, it is my own turn, as I near the stump.

I face the axman. I put my head on the stump, and wait for it to be chopped off. The axman raises his ax, and then begins his downward, deadly trace. I, Joseph Gavi, wait.

And then I wake up, tense and drenched with sweat. It is a dream! Only a dream!

But it is a dream that has far too many realistic qualities and proportions. It is 1941, and Joseph Gavi lives in Minsk, Byelorussia, in the Union of the Soviet Socialist Republics. While he is dreaming, the Germans are planning to come into his region, and he knows from listening to conversations of the grown-ups around him that Germans are fiercely anti-Semitic, very much in fact like the Soviet government under which he and his family live.

It is a dream to come true all too soon.

JOSEPH

My family probably came from some place in Poland.[2] My mother was Rachel and her father, Kiva Paley, was a businessman before the 1917 revolution. He had a shop selling leather from cowskin, and he employed ten to fifteen people in the village of Smilovichi, about twenty miles from Minsk. He was a Jewish Capitalist and not permitted to live in the big city.

[2] That is, of course, the Russian part of Poland. Historically, Poland had been divided among Russia, Prussia, and Austria. Poland as an independent country did not come back into existence until after World War I.

He told me once that the authorities ask 'where the old gold is' (presumably that he had hidden before the revolution), and imprisoned him for four weeks when he could not, or would not, tell them. Just as suddenly as the NKVD (secret police) took him, they let him go. Did he prove that he had no gold? If he had any, did he say so? I never found out, nor did any other member of my family.

I visited Smilovichi every September and October, where I helped grandfather Kiva to store apples in straw in the attic to keep them from rotting in the upcoming winters. Grandfather also taught me how to fish in a nearby river. He made little toys that he gave to me and the other children, much to our delight.

My paternal grandfather, Shaya Gavi, also ran a small business in pre-revolutionary times; he made envelopes, and was allowed, unlike Kiva, to remain inside the Minsk city limits. Just why, no one could ever explain. His 'position,' however, did not exempt him years later, when the Russians, his own countrymen, condemned him for being a Capitalist. And, certainly, as will be shown, he was not exempt from the horrors of the holocaust.

The early, or revolutionary Communists confiscated just about everything Joseph's grandparents on both sides of the family possessed. Along with the confiscation came the loss of the right to vote or to be accepted in any college or university throughout the country; the only thing left for them was physical labor. Why? Because they were Jews. Or Capitalists. Or both. These confiscations caused Kiva and Hannah Paley, Rachel's parents, to give up their holdings in Smilovichi and move to Minsk, where Kiva got a job in a toy factory.

JOSEPH   From my mother Rachel's side of the family, there was Uncle Sholem, a supply clerk in a local factory, and Aunt Liza, who got married and moved to Leningrad.

My father was Naum. His brother, uncle Isaac, played professional chess and frequently judged chess tournaments. He visits each Saturday for our sabbath supper, and tells such stories to me and the other children in the family that all of us had to go make a pee beforehand.

After the meal Isaac always lies down on a sofa and asks us 'Where did we leave off last time?' And then he told us about princesses and princes and fairies and trips on the sea. All the stories ended the same way: the good characters always won and the bad ones were punished.[3]

My uncle David Gavi was a bookkeeper. Aunt Polia comes from my father's side, as did Aunt Fanya, and Aunt Manya, who had two children, Isia and Sarah, who played with me in the streets of Minsk in the time just before the war. All of my relatives except Mama, younger brother Leva (born February 25, 1941) Uncle Isaac and Aunt Liza, were killed by the Germans during their occupation of Minsk.

The two families were moved by the authorities, right at war's beginning, to the little neighborhood of Grushevski-Poselok, about two miles from the center of Minsk, into a two-story barracks-like structure. On each floor there were eight different families. Joseph, Rachel, Naum, and Rachel's parents, lived in a two-room ground floor apartment that altogether measured about two hundred square feet. Kiva and Hannah lived in one room, while Joseph, his parents, and, later, Leva, the other. On the second floor, in an identical apartment, the entire family on Naum's side lived.

JOSEPH   My grandfathers, Kiva Paley and Shaya Gavi, were serious, religious men. Both were strict with us children, and almost never make any jokes. But my grandmother, Hannah, was a jovial woman who slept in a huge bed (at least huge to us children) with pillows and covers made of goose down. Frequently, all of us come in from the outside and collectively jump into grandmother's bed and frolic around, to the annoyance of grandfather and the amusement of grandmother.

My father, Naum, was an opera singer, performing in the large cities. While at home he sang in a synagogue choir before the revolution, and later frequently took me with him to his practice sessions. In 1935, just before I was four years old, in November, Papa took me to music school where I studied violin for the next five years. Well before I entered regular school, I was a somewhat accomplished violinist.

---

[3] Isaac settled in Brest after the war, but soon lost his vision. He continued to lead an active chess life, turning his apartment into an amateur chess club. He died in 1979. One of his sons, Ilia, became a physician; the other, Leva, a mechanical engineer.

My young life was happy, satisfying, and fulfilling. I was very close to my father, as I frequently played the violin while he sang arias from the operas he performed.

Papa never raised his voice at me; he never spanked me. Mama was more strict than Papa; nevertheless, neither I nor the other children ever heard them argue with one another.

Joseph came from a home that was socially and culturally dignified, one that showed the greatest respect for education and learning. His was a world of great literature, music, and poetry. He did not start regular schooling until he was eight years old – in 1940. (Seven was the average beginning age). Some health problems caused Naum to hold Joseph out of the public schools for as long as he possibly could. Maybe it was a case of Naum just not wanting to let go of Joseph, and turn him over to the public authorities, in this case, the schoolteachers.

In any event, Joseph found that he had to grow up in a hurry. He had barely finished the first grade when war broke out between Germany and the Soviet Union. Because of the war, Joseph led a very different life from the one which had been envisioned for him by Rachel and Naum, and by Joseph himself.[4]

In 1939, when Joseph turned eight, Germany and the Soviet Union divided Poland (which had regained its independence only at the end of World War I). This division caused a huge influx of Jewish refugees from Poland to pour into Byelorussia, especially to towns of any size like Gomel, Pinsk, Vitebsk, and Minsk, all in an effort to avoid rule by the Nazis.

Many of Naum's kinfolk were among the new arrivals. A few of these relatives were members of the Polish Communist party; because of this status, the local Soviet authorities gave them jobs and housing. A scant year later, however, in 1940, they were arrested and taken to gulags around the country. The charge? They had had contacts with foreigners, mostly Poles, but also with Englishmen. By 1940 the paranoid Soviet government considered that if you ever had any connection with a foreign power, or

---

[4] Unknown to him at the time, a seven-year-old girl, Ida Engels, his future wife, was evacuated out of Minsk to Chvalensk on the Volga River. Her cousin, August (whose mother was American) accompanied her. Years after the war, Ida had no trace of where August was, and so she presumed him to be dead.

But then in 1977 Ida found him. He had thought through all these years that his entire family had been wiped out; he did not even know that he was Jewish in origin. Finally, August came to Minsk to meet Ida and Joseph, and their family. He walked around and around their apartment for one entire day without knocking or otherwise letting them know he was there. He was anxious about ending the life he had always known, and literally starting all over again. He died a few years later, a victim to cancer, but nonetheless as much a casualty of war as anyone. His was just one of millions of sad deaths associated with World War II.

with any of its people, you were a potential spy and should be prosecuted.

Most of the people from Naum's Polish side of the family were left to fend for themselves; three additional families moved into the already crowded apartment where Joseph lived. With so many refugees coming in from Poland to escape the Nazis, and with the mixed reception the Soviet authorities gave them, the Minsk ghetto was already well in the making by the time the Germans invaded Russia in June of 1941.

Naum was on a concert trip to Brest, when foreign minister Vyacheslav Molotov broadcast to the nation that the Germans were attacking. Everyone, it seemed, tried to leave the big cities, including Minsk.

JOSEPH My mother, Rachel, however, cannot go anywhere, since she has given birth to Leva only three months before. My family and I, we watch the German air strikes on Minsk from our neighborhood of Grushevski-Poselok, a few meters away. There are miles and miles of fire in the sky as the German aircraft – thirty or forty each hour, or so it seemed – bomb the city.

We, along with our neighbors at Grushevski-Poselok, had dug trenches, expecting a German air attack. When the German bombers came, we hid in these trenches, and 'miraculously' were not hit. There was no resistance from the Soviet air force against these German air attacks. Nor was there resistance when German soldiers marched into Minsk directly after the air attacks stopped. Many of our neighbors feel the same way grandfather Kiva does. He says: 'I am not worried about the Germans. They were nice people during the occupation in 1918, certainly better than the Communists.' There is never a thought by any member of my family of fleeing Minsk because of the German occupation. Both our families are distrustful of Communism, and definitely, the Germans can't be any worse; probably a great deal better.

Kiva and people of his generation remembered the Germans of World War I as being "civilized." One of the most excruciating questions for Kiva, Shaya, and other older Russians in World War II was "how did the Germans change so drastically from one war to another?" This was, for them, an essentially un-answerable question, but they did continue to make sharp distinctions between the regular German soldier and the Nazi SS. The former, they argued, had no choices but to follow the hateful orders of the latter.

For the first few days after the German occupation of Minsk began – on June 28, 1941, five months before his tenth birthday – Joseph and his family lay low. Naum, having returned from west Byelorussia at the height of the fighting to see to his family, told Joseph not to go anywhere, or he would be killed.

Nevertheless, young Joseph and a friend wandered into the areas surrounding Grushevski-Poselok and saw German troops, some of whom gave candy to the youths. These soldiers were "normal" and friendly, giving Joseph the impression that perhaps grandfather was right; maybe the Germans were better than the Communists. But these were regular soldiers; Joseph had yet to meet the SS or political police.

Supplies ran low. The Gavi family as well as many of their neighbors (Jews and non-Jews alike) decided they would have to risk going into town to find food. And this procedure was not as dreadful – at least the first time – as many had originally feared. There was no place to buy anything, but stores were open, with people taking bread, oil, wheat, and many other commodities without payment; in short, they were allowed to stock up for possibly bad days ahead. Joseph and a friend found an open warehouse full of boots. He grabbed a couple of them and ran off. Later, at home, he found they were both left footed.

The Germans permitted this "near-looting" to go on for four or five days. Then they began to put people in a line, telling them to take only what they could personally hold. (Watching the line, Joseph thought of the dream he had been having lately). Apparently this German leniency was intended to make the Jews of Minsk feel that they were liked and would be well treated. Once word of this "benevolence" got around, they believed increasing numbers of Jews would come out of hiding and could thus be dealt with. To an alarming degree, these suppositions turned out to be true.

For example, on about the tenth day of the occupation, signs appeared on all the city's walls that on a certain date all men between seventeen and fifty would have to come to Shirokaya Street in central Minsk. Some others were ordered to a prisoner of war camp on Drozdy Plaza. Anyone failing to follow these orders would be hunted down by German soldiers and Byelorussian police, wearing "helmets decorated with skulls and metal discs," and shot.

Uncle Isaac suddenly disappeared from Minsk, and was not heard of again for a long time. Was he shot? Did he slip out to Moscow? (As it turned out, he was almost blind, and was relieved of military duties. See footnote three). Uncle David was in the house, and he did go to Shirokaya Street, and stayed there for four excruciating days.

The weather turned extremely hot in July 1941 throughout much of the Soviet Union, including Minsk. About 7,000 men were ordered to sit or lie down in the plaza and not move. On each corner of the plaza German guards with machine guns shot anybody who stood up, or, for that matter, moved very much in their sitting position.

One observer noted: "The slightest attempt to make oneself comfortable was met with a bullet. Death was the price of a moistened throat."[5]

The men went the whole four days without food or drink. Some of them, in desperation, tried to drink the urine that seeped out over the hot pavement, while others suffered sunstroke and heart attacks. No food or water were distributed by the German guards, but "thousands of women, with bottles of water and patties made of potato flour" surreptitiously and with bribes "repeatedly broke through the guards and gave the food and drink to the prisoners."[6]

After nearly a week, the Germans let the majority of these Russian Jews go; just told them to go home – at least whatever homes they now had. In mid-July other posters appeared saying that "All Jewish people must move to certain parts of the city" laid out for them by the German authorities.

The Minsk Jews, and those from surrounding areas, were moved to the western part of the city, where the Germans fenced off Nemiga Street, Ubileynaya Plaza (meaning "Jubilee," but ultimately called by the Minsk Jews "Slavery Square")[7] and several other thoroughfares, putting as many as sixty and seventy people in each of the houses that stood alongside it.

This was the first activity, or "Aktion," as the Germans put it, toward building what became the Minsk ghetto; the Germans called it a "Jewish residential district,"[8] with some 100,000 local Jews in confinement.

JOSEPH   It is not a concentration camp, but a death camp. Concentration camps have some supplies, whereas ghetto has none. Also, the Concentration camps contained people of differ-

[5] For additional information on this event, plus others having to do with the Minsk ghetto, see Hersh Smoliar, The Minsk Ghetto, trans. by Hyman J. Lewbin. Oakland, CA: Judah L. Magnes Memorial Museum, 1966. p. 1. Also see Shalom Cholavsky, "The German Jews in the Minsk Ghetto," Yad Vasham Studies, No. 17; 1986, pp. 219-249.
[6] Reuben Ainsztein, Jewish Resistance in Nazi-Occupied Eastern Europe (New York: Barnes and Noble, 1974), 463-485.
[7] Smoliar, 11.
[8] Smoliar, 5.

ent nationalities and ghettos only Jews. Term ghetto associates with the concentration on the particular territory of the group of people of any nationality. At the same time, Jewish ghetto on the occupied territory was in essence an interim station before final extermination of the Jewish inhabitants. Therefore, a term 'extermination camps' would be a more appropriate description to reflect essence of the Jewish ghetto on the territory of Belarus, Poland, and Ukraine.

When my family – and also all the other families-from the ghetto, we take only those household furnishings we could carry – only what we could hold in our two hands. So, a great many things of value were left behind. One was Papa's 'machorka,' or smoking tobacco. This could be used, not just to satisfy Papa's nicotine habit but also to trade for food and supplies.

I hid the machorka in our old apartment; I put it in with my toys so no one would see it. Several days after arriving at the ghetto, with Papa wanting a smoke, I slip out and returned to the old apartment and brought the machorka back with me. This was risky business, because the Germans had already announced that any Jew found outside the ghetto would be shot on sight.

I was small, though, not even five feet tall, and I had a better chance of slipping, undetected, under the barbed-wire fences than any other member of the family. Of course, I was scared. Who would not have been? I could be stopped by unfriendly non-Jews and turned in to the German authorities.

I wait until dark before going out; on the way to and from the apartment I hide from everybody, learning to slink behind buildings and bushes, to make a constant cover for myself. Unknowingly, I am training myself for later work in rescuing ghetto residents and leading them to the partisans in the nearby forests.

Additional streets were soon cordoned off for the ghetto. In addition to Nemiga, Respublikanskaya, Obuwnaya, Sherokay (where the Gavis lived), Suchaya, and Ostrovskaya streets were closed in by barbed wire. The entire area was in the vicinity of the Minsk Jewish cemetery. There was no central water supply, just a few wells scattered here and there where residents gathered to use a hand-operated pump to get water.

Personal cleanliness quickly went by the board – because any water that could be found had to be used for drinking and – whatever that was under the circumstances – cooking. Simple matters of personal hygiene, such as brushing one's teeth, and cleansing one's hair, became forlorn hopes. Though in scattered places, ghetto residents were allowed to build crude, wooden latrines, men, women, and children soon learned that they had to relieve their bodies' calls of nature wherever and whenever they happened to be: in the street in front of God and the world, or in an outback alley. The embarrassment that earlier would have devastated these ghetto residents was soon lost in the horrible mess that was the Minsk ghetto. A change of clothes was only something that had happened in a previous life. Laundering was usually out of the question, and shirts and pants were worn until they became mere rags. The inability to stay clean and hygenic only added to the health problems and miseries caused by the bestial and despicable German occupiers and their Byelorussian collaborators.

There was little supply of food, medicine, or indeed, anything in the ghetto. A "free-market" began operating just outside the ghetto, across the fences. The Jews inside the ghetto went to the fence to exchange gold, silver, clothes, shoes and boots, and other valuable belongings with free Russians on the outside. Aunt Manya went to the fence one day, and was trading for potatoes, onions, and bread. A German guard spotted her, and shot her dead.

Despite the obvious dangers, trading at the fence continued. It had to. Otherwise, the ghetto occupants would have starved to death.

JOSEPH

Grandfather Shaya had a gold pocket watch, given to him many years before by his own grandfather. It was of great sentimental value to him. After the family had traded everything it had, it came down to grandfather's watch. He refused to give it to the family. Only when some members of the family threatened to take it from him by force, did he begin to weep, and hand it over. As It was, it only brought in a few slices of bread.

Mama herself went to the fence on some occasions. Once, she met an old man on the other side, who mysteriously opened a metal box, and in it were diamonds – thousands of them, or so it seemed. He gave half a dozen to Mama and told her to exchange them for food.

Asking around after this man, we learned that he had been a wealthy businessman before the Revolution, in the fur trade, but for some unknown reasons the Communists had never apprehended him. He was obviously using his fortune for good works before being shot by either the Germans or the Russians.

In the center of the rapidly developing Minsk ghetto was Plaza Ubileynaya. Here was the old Minsk city police building, as well as an old barn. The barn became a daytime prison where people who had tried to escape during the day were kept until nightfall, when they were taken to the cemetery and shot. No effort was made to capture any nighttime escapees: they were shot immediatley, with no questions asked. Also, German troops and Jewish policemen sought out many old people and children in the ghetto, as well as those who were infirm, and took them to the barn during the day, to await their executions.

In the old police building, a Judenrat was established, at the suggestion of the chief of civil administration in Byelorussia, Wilhelm Kube. The Judenrat was supposedly like a "city hall" for the ghetto, ostensibly to give the Jews a semblance of autonomy, or at least tried to make them believe they had some kind of self-government. Unfortunately, it was a show, a ruse, perpetrated by the Germans for possible international inspections.

Nothing could have been more deceiving, since the Jewish police roamed the ghetto, spotting any discipline or trouble spots and reporting these incidents to the Nazi authorities. (Even before the war ended, many of the "Jewish policemen" paid dearly for their Nazi collaborations. They were all killed in 1943 when the Minsk ghetto was terminated. Even if they had been able to escape from the ghetto, their fate would have been the same at the hands of the Russian partisans).

In addition to the Jewish police, the Judenrat provided a postal service, a food and housing distribution facility, and a health organization – at least, of sorts. In no instance were the Jews in the Minsk ghetto (or, for that matter the ghettos in other cities) given any kind of freedom. All of the talk about "autonomy" and "self-government" was nothing but cynical propaganda from the Nazis.

Fortunately for the residents of the Minsk ghetto, Eliyahu Mushkin was appointed chairman of their Judenrat. A native of Minsk and an engineer by profession, Mushkin established contact with the ghetto Underground (headed by Isai Pavlovich Kazinets) and helped Jews escape to join the partisans. "Mushkin was able to warn the Underground of impending dangers, and the Jews respected him."[9]

---

[9] See Mushkin, Eliyahu," in Encyclopedia of the Holocaust, 3 (New York: Macmillana Publishing, 1990), 1021-1022.

Obviously, Mushkin had to walk a tightrope between seeing to the welfare of the Minsk Jews and at least appearing to adhere to German directives. Mushkin was ultimately arrested by the Germans, and in early 1942, was tortured and hanged to death.

Kube[10] convinced the Germans that all able bodied men should be put to work in various factories around Minsk. The largest of these was the Voroshilov machine factory, where German tanks damaged on the front were repaired.

Old people, women, and children were required to stay in the ghetto while their husbands, sons, and fathers worked in the factories. Usually 100 of them – sometimes up to 300 – would be herded together during the day, taken to the barn on Ubileynay Plaza, kept there until night fell, and then taken to the Jewish cemetery and shot.

The able bodied men working in the German factories got more food and drink than those left behind in the ghetto. At least they could keep up their strength – plus, they had contact with the free Russian population, giving them the opportunity of exchanging various things for food and medications. But if they were hurt on the job, or fell ill, they were taken to the barn and then the cemetery, where they were killed.

Back at the ghetto, "flea markets" cropped up on one little plaza after another. Though they were ostensibly illegal, the Jewish police overlooked these trading centers, where the Minsk Jews among themselves traded valuables for what little food was available. The "markets" along the fences continued, also, between the ghetto residents and free Russians outside.

As the Germans had announced in trying to sound benevolent, an old school was turned into a "hospital" within the confines of the Minsk ghetto. What they did not say was that there were no physicians for this hospital other than a few Jewish doctors who volunteered their time. And, of course, there was no medicine. And every two or three weeks a group of gestapo thugs would drink too much, disguise themselves as doctors, hide machine guns under their gowns and storm into the hospital, killing every patient in sight. Many Jews died jumping from the third floor hospital window to get away from the despicable Nazis.

Word spread of these hospital atrocities throughout the ghetto, which helped two things to happen. First, naturally, fewer ill people went to the hospital. And second, it caused many of the Minsk Jews to become resistance fighters. The feeling was that "the ghetto means death. Provide

---

[10] Later, Kube was killed by his own maid, a Byelorussian partisan named E.G. Mazanik. She placed a bomb under his bed. See Encyclopaedia Judica, v. 12; p. 56

36

yourself with arms, leave the ghetto and take to the forests!"[11] In most instances, as the saying goes, this was easier said than done.

Perhaps it was this growing resistance – a Jewish saying was "if our fate is to perish, let it be on the battlefield" – that caused the first major assault against the Minsk Jews. It happened in August 1941 and before it ended, some 5,000 Jews lay dead at German hands.

Early one morning, the German guards marched dozens of men, not to the factories, but to a place outside of town, and had them dig trenches. Even then, they did not think anything was too unusual; just that instead of working in the factory on this day they would dig trenches, for whatever purpose the Germans had in mind.

Of course, the diggers were shot. Then the Germans marched literally hundreds of other people: men, women, and children, out of the ghetto, shot them and buried them collectively in the trenches. Some, it was later reported, were still alive when they were buried by tons of earth.

By November 1941, the Minsk Jews at last realized their plight: that the Germans were their mortal enemy, and they began to prepare for future atrocities. They installed escape places, called "malenas," in each house. Sometimes this entailed building a double wall where residents could hide during a pogrom (an event in which not only Germans but native Byelorussians participated). More frequently, however, it was digging trenches under each house's floor, and tunnels under the streets. Once these were completed, food and water sufficient for at least four days were stored in them.

JOSEPH   My father, Naum, built a malena, a tiny trench under the floor, where our family hoped we could hide in another attack. And on November 6, 1941, drunken Nazis once again stormed through the streets of the Minsk ghetto.

Our malena was not used on this particular occasion. Living with us at the time was a former Minsk policeman named Sukenek. 'If they come,' he said, 'I will not go to the malena. I will kill myself with a razor blade.'

Mama could not go to the malena, because Leva was seven months old, and surely he would scream, and this would alert the Nazis to our location. Papa vowed to stay with Mama, and I would not be separated from my beloved parents. Thus we all stayed in the house, waiting for the worst. We heard shooting and screaming.

---

[11] Ainsztein, Jewish Resistance, 463.

I peek out of a shutter. I see people being taken from their houses and shot right in the middle of the street. I see a crazed old woman run through the street furiously shaking a pillow, the feathers flying all around her. Taunting her are two Byelorussian policemen who are Nazi collaborators.

A little boy of three or so is running, screaming for his mother. A couple of gestapo thugs catch him by the legs and crush his skull against a wall before my eyes and then just drop his little body right onto the street.

Somewhere around the Ostrovsky Street archway (so I heard later), a Jewish inmate went to the head of the street, and with a machine gun began to kill Nazis. He got about a dozen before they killed him. 'Some hero,' was the ghetto judgment. Right after the Germans killed Jews or took them off to be killed, Russians and Byelorussians alike walked into their homes to loot the abandoned personal belongings and furniture. We don't know where they are going to stop, or how many they will kill.

As I watch the Nazis get closer and closer to my home, I feel a working on my body, with terrible itching and burning. I reach inside my shirt and bring out two handsful of a wriggling mass. I have never seen such a thing before, so I ask my father, 'Papa, what is this?'

Papa knows what these little creatures are that I am holding in my hand – they are lice – and he feels so frustrated and helpless at this moment that he breaks down and cries. He hugs Mama, Leva, and me, and in a close embrace, my family waits for them to come and kill us.

But then, as suddenly as it started, the horror ended. The very next house would have been the one where the Gavis lived. Apparently the Nazis were not working for any particular quota to kill. Instead, they were shrinking the ghetto. After killing everyone from a certain block, or taking them off to be gassed – generally at a place some twelve kilometers from Minsk named Maly Trostinetz – the Germans would then move the fences, decreasing the size of the camp.

Joseph heard later that many from the ghetto were taken to Ubileynaya Plaza, where upon arriving, they thought a feast was in progress. They were correct: there was a feast, but not for them. The SS men lined up tables and loaded them down with food and alcohol, and obviously en-joyed themselves as they watched guards roughly pushing helpless people into death trucks. There was even an orchestra playing three-quarter time German waltzes and marches. (Sometime later, one of the victims, a well-known opera singer from Minsk, and friend of Naum Gavi, began loudly to sing various arias, and tried to get the band to follow him. He became – perhaps mercifully so – completely disoriented by the time he climbed aboard a death truck).

Near the SS festivities, a long line of people waited to be placed in trucks to be taken on work details, or so they thought. As soon as the trucks moved out with some fifty to sixty people aboard, their internal exhaust systems poured into the closed-in vehicles. Only then did the Jews from the Minsk ghetto realize what was happening to them, as they banged fiercely on the walls and gasped for breath. They were, of course, all dead by the time they reached Maly Trostinetz. Then the trucks returned to Ubileynaya Plaza to pick up more Jews in the midst of the German feast and music.

It appeared that the reason for this in early November was to clear an area for incoming Jews from Germany, Austria, Poland, Czechoslova-kia, and other east European countries. On November 8, 990 Jews from Hamburg arrived in Minsk and occupied the houses of those Minsk Jews who had been murdered on the two previous days. Soon afterward, Jews from Dusseldorf, Frankfurt, Berlin, Bremen, and Vienna arrived, further complicating an already difficult situation. Commissar Kube protested – to no avail – these newcomers from the west, saying that he could not assimi-late them, for according to gestapo directive they all had to live separately from the Minsk Jews.[12] Also, though Kube was fiercely anti-Semitic, he did protest the presence of certain Jews from Germany. Apparently, there were numerous German Jewish veterans of World War I who could prove their services to the "Fatherland' in earlier times. Kube wanted them saved, a request that meant nothing to the Nazi overlords.[13] Angrily, he told them that their actions were "unworthy of a German and the Germany of Kant and Goethe."[14]

There were now the "Reich" or "protectorate" Jews in the ghetto (from Germany and Austria – altogether some 7,000 persons) and the "Minsk" or "Russian" Jews, 90,000 to 100,000 in number. "Barbed wire fences blocked

---

[12] See Cholavsky, 220-221.

[13] See Gerald Reitlinger, The Final Solution: The Attempt to Exterminate the Jews of Europe, 1939-1945 (New York: A.S. Barnes & Co., 1953), 223-227.

[14] Ibid, 288.

the passage leading from the Russian ghetto to the Reich Jews' ghetto and transit from one to the other was prohibited. Respublikanskaya Street formed the border between the two."[15]

Even though the Minsk Jews outnumbered the "western" Jews twelve to one, the policy continued of killing and transporting out the Russians to make way for Germans and Austrians, and ultimately Czechs. Thus on November 21 another "aktion" occurred, and if anything, it was worse than the one on the 6th and 7th.

JOSEPH This time the gestapo started shrinking the ghetto on the other side from where my family and I lived; fortunately for us, we lived almost in the center of the ghetto. Nevertheless, there was much uncertainty: will they reach us this time? Should we go to the malena? Will our entire family be annihilated? Will we suffer?

On this occasion, Mama took matters into her own hands. She decided that she would somehow slip out of the ghetto, and take Leva back to our old apartment. At the same time, she insisted that Papa and I go into the malena and stay there until the terror ended.

When we were forced to enter the Minsk ghetto, Papa had offered our apartment in Grushevski-Poselok to a singing colleague, who had accompanied him on opera tours. Papa thought the move to the 'Jewish residential district' was only temporary, and soon we would all come back home. The apartment was fully furnished, and the friend and his wife and children were grateful for Papa's generosity.

Mother – as she related to me and Papa later – went to one of the few 'official' gates to the ghetto, and waited for the guards to be distracted long enough for her and Leva to slip through, and thus at least momentarily escape the horrors of the ghetto. She walked four miles, with Leva held tightly to her – zigzagging across an entire city with an anti-Semitic population ready to turn her in to the police and a certain death. Tired and hungry, she found our old apartment, and knocked on the door. At last, the opera singer's wife answered, and immediately recognized my mother, Rachel, and my brother, Leva. She shouted, 'You dirty Jews; go back to your ghetto, or I'll call the police and have you arrested!'

[15] Cholavsky 222.

Wearily, Mama and Leva wandered around in the night. If they had been caught by the Germans or the Byelorussian Police, they would have been tortured and killed. Fortunately, it was a dark night, and they eluded the patrols. Unfortunately, however, the darkness caused Mama to lose her way several times, and it took her until next morning early to get back to our house in the ghetto. While Leva slept soundly, thank God, Mama slipped under the fence, and made her way, hungry and exhausted, 'home.'

We had no legal right to the old apartment, but the present occupants' attitude hurt us very badly. Papa and he had been long-time friends. Mama and Papa rationalized that the woman was probably just scared. If anyone hid Jews who had escaped from the ghetto, they would be killed or imprisoned, or even moved to the ghetto themselves. It was all a matter of self-preservation.

In the "aktions" of 7 and 21 November, 1941, some 20,000 people, all of whom were Jews, were slaughtered by the German occupiers. This number included a group of scantily clad Russian prisoners of war (Jewish and non-Jewish), many of whom died of the cold as they were marched into Minsk. They had been taken prisoners at the battles of Vyazma and Moscow.[16]

If a man did not move fast enough," the savage guards opened fire on him," and this aktion continued throughout the night. The next day, ghetto residents could see "frozen rivers of blood," and "mountains of frozen bodies."[17]

The sight caused many emotions to rise, and anger was one of them. The continual aktions, but especially those of November and December of 1941, caused more than one Minsk Jew to raise his fist in anger. Symbolically, that raised fist marked the end of German domination over the Russians.

---

[16] Ainsztein, Jewish Resistance, 469.
[17] Smoliar, 27.

CHAPTER TWO

THE HOLOCAUST STRIKES HOME

JOSEPH Each day Papa and I leave the ghetto for the Voroshilov tank repair factory. At least there we get soup and enough bread to slip back to Mama and Leva, who had to stay behind in the ghetto. Papa works with a group repairing windows and other glass fixtures in the factory.

I come into contact with so many Germans during the building of the Minsk ghetto that even after less than a year I learned to speak their language. The Germans assigned me to the plumbing department, but I acted primarily as an interpreter between the German occupiers and the Russian prisoners of war who made up most of the labor force for the factory. They lived in several large barracks, while Papa and I marched every day in columns back to the ghetto.

The Soviet prisoners, I learned, were strictly separated in the barracks: Who is Jew? Who is Communist? Who is gypsy? And many were routinely executed – usually by hanging – for some infraction, such as stealing a potato, or talking back to a guard. Papa and I had not been working at the factory even for a week until we saw ten to fifteen people hanging on scaffolds in the courtyard. And they hung there for three days as an object lesson for all the other prisoners.

The German officer in charge of this plumbing shop liked me. Unlike so many of his fellow soldiers, he was a normal human being, and he behaved like one. He was not strict with the Russian prisoners, never raising his voice or striking them. He frequently put me on his lap, and actually said that he sympathized with the plight of the Russian people. The German soldier brought extra bread for me to take back to the ghetto, and gave me full freedom of the shop, and even the factory, without any kind of restrictions. I could go anywhere without trouble from the Germans.

In my conversations with the Russian prisoners who worked in the boiler room – where I came each day to warm up, to bake a potato in the fire, and to talk – the subject very often got around to escape (it is now early winter, 1942), and the work of the partisans against the Germans. 'We need civilian clothes,' one of them said to me. 'We cannot escape in our army uniforms. We would quickly be detected and shot,' one of them said to me.

'I can supply you with civilian clothes,' I assured them, 'but only if you promise to take me with you to the partisans.'

'Sure kid,' the prisoner replied easily. 'We will take you with us, and you will learn the way to the partisans and come back and save your family.'

Over the next several days in the ghetto, piece by piece, from Kiva's and Shaya's wardrobes and from neighbors, I gathered up enough clothes for two of the prisonerss to wear in their escape. These 'new' clothes worked just fine; it gave the two men the kind of identity that would be the most helpful in getting away from the German encampment.

But now they wanted pistols, two or three of them if possible, but at least one. 'Without guns we cannot make it,' they told me. One day I saw my chance. While tanks were being worked on during the day, the drivers and other crewmembers stayed close to supervise. Each day at lunch, though, they pulled off their gun belts, and put them up on the tank so they would not be bothered with them at mealtime. As I looked over the area, I found a belt that still had a pistol in it!

I shake with excitement as I near the gun. I know that if I am seen, there will be serious consequences. Certainly, no fatherly paddling for a mischievous young boy! It will be a German bullet through the brain.

I pick up the pistol and head straightway for the plumbing shop. I stash it in an air duct, and put some old wrappings – newspapers and old rags and such – over it, not only to keep it from view but from possibly being moved around as well.

About 12:30 p.m., the Germans discovered that the firearm was missing. They ordered all prisoners and workers from the ghetto (over 2,000 of us) out onto the plaza in freezing cold weather and for the next twenty-four hours they searched us for the missing weapon. All through the night, without food and water and only scantily clad, we prisoners and workers stood as German guards shouted over and over: 'Wo ist der pistole? Wo ist der pistole?'

I don't say, of course, where the gun is. They don't find it. The next day it is over; they stop looking and let everyone back into the ghettos. Under the circumstances of the freezing weather, even the old barracks for POWs and ghetto residents who had been forced to stay overnight, look good to all of us.

I did tell Papa what I had done. Papa was pleased. 'It's not a big deal,' we agreed, 'because either way,' Papa said fatalistically, 'we're going to die. We can die here in the factory, or we can die trying to regain our dignity and freedom.' This way, I had at least a faint chance of getting out, of escaping to the partisans. Papa is happy for me to do this.

I slip the gun out of the plumbing room where I have hidden it, and carefully bring it to the two Russians. I whisper to Papa that today the prisoners are escaping and I am going with them, so Papa should not look for me soon.

The two prisoners discarded their uniforms and put on the civilian clothes I had brought them. One of them pocketed the gun. For some reason, they knew they were going to be marched away from encampment that day, to do some work outside the city. They, along with myself, got into one of the inside columns so we would not easily be noticeable to the German guards, either accompanying the march or at the various checkpoints along the way.

When we got to Mogilev Road, the columns went left and my two colleagues and I slipped away and off to the right. We walked eastward on Mogilev Road for about an hour and a half and then one of the prisoners said to me: 'Joseph, you have to go back.'

'Why?' I incredulously asked.

'Because you are such a little kid, and you might hold us back.'

'I will not.'

'We can't take the chance.'

I start to cry, and one of the Russians slaps me. Both lost their tempers and, forgetting how and why they were on the road to freedom themselves, they beat me back, though I had been their benefactor.

It seemed that everyone who dreamed of escape from the ghetto, barracks, or factory, wanted to join the partisans and fight against the Germans. What they did not realize at first was that the Russian partisans were just as fiercely anti-Semitic as, or perhaps even more, than their German torturers.[18]

In reality, I learned an important lesson from this experience with the two prisoners. Increasingly, I realized that, even at my tender age, I was quite on my own in an unfriendly world.

Well before he was a teenager, Joseph Gavi had grown to manhood.

He did, to be sure, join the partisans at a later date, but even then, the only bond that held him to them was their common hatred of Germans and their intentions to do them harm at every opportunity. Joseph grew to distrust the partisans and for that matter just about everyone else who did not belong to his immediate family.

JOSEPH   I slipped back into the ghetto at about midnight. Everyone was disappointed that I had not made good on my effort to flee the grasp of the Germans. I went back to the factory and rejoined Papa, working in and around the tank repair shop. The authorities never did learn of my theft of the pistol and my attempt to escape.

---

[18] Anna Krasnoperko confirmed this anti-Semitism among the partisans in an interview she gave to the Moscow Times November 5, 1993: "no one from the ghetto was accepted by partisans..." In a partisan controlled village, a drunken man drew a revolver at newly arriving Jews and loudldy asked them: "Did you poison the wells?"

As usual, on the morning of March 2, 1942 – the day of Purim, celebrating the defeat of Haman the Amalekite – Papa and I went to the building that housed the Judenrat, where the columns with workers were formed – to be marched on to the Voroshilov factory. Just before joining the column, Papa told me that he was to join a different column today and work in a place where perhaps it was easier to exchange things for food. He instructed me to go to the Voroshilov Factory, and if Papa's new place really was easier, he would send for me.

Did I see a glint in Papa's eyes this morning? Did Papa sense that this was the last time he would ever see me and the rest of his family?

That evening, the Germans did not let anyone go back to the ghetto; they ordered all workers to stay in the POW camp – on the same street as the factory. And the authorities kept them there for three endless days, without any explanation or information about their families. Everyone speculated that the only reasons they were not marched back to the ghetto was because something terrible back there must be happening. And they were right.

JOSEPH   At dusk on the fourth day the Germans let me go, free to return to the ghetto. I go home, and the first thing I see is my grandmother, Hannah, peacefully reposed on the stoop – shot dead by the Germans, or so I automatically assumed.

As I heard it related to me some time afterward, it was one of those times when drunken German soldiers and Byelorussian policemen came through the ghetto, looking for any Jew they could find. They entered my household, and grandmother Hannah, ill with fever and diarrhea, stayed in bed. The thugs found her and shot her in bed where she lay ill and then took her out of the house and threw her onto the stoop.

Grandfather Kiva was in the same room when Hannah was shot. He fled to a corner where a large pile of dirty clothes was stacked, full of lice, and smelling bad. The murderers were afraid to get too close to the clothes.

Mama and Leva had also been in the house when the criminals arrived. She took Leva upstairs to the attic. There were piles of clothes here, as well as books, and other matter. She went inside the junk with Leva under her arms. She heard the shot that killed Hannah, but did not know until later just how deadly it had been.

The soldiers climbed the stairs to the attic, and started to search for anyone who might be hiding. They used rifle-cleaning rods to stick into clothes piles. Mama wrapped one-year-old Leva tightly to her chest, and he made not one sound during the ten minute search. It was pure chance that the rifle rods didn't touch her and her infant. Finally, after many agonizing moments she heard one of the soldiers say, 'There is nobody here. We've at least killed one, and nobody's left. Let's go.'

Mama knew this was what the soldier said, for he spoke it in the Byelorussian language. She knew then, most depresssingly so, that her own countrymen were trying to kill her!

Carrying Leva on her side, Mama finally went downstairs to find her father, Kiva, weeping, and her mother, Hannah, dead on the stoop.

During the same slaughter, March 1942, everyone went into a malena at grandfather Shaya's house except the grandfather himself. A religious man, he had nailed a mezuza on the jamb of his front door, following a Jewish tradition of thousands of years. It was a sign or symbol made of a parchment scroll with texts from Deuteronomy on one side and the "Shaddai" on the other, to help in getting God to remember and protect the individual who put it up. Shaya believed that if he stood under the mezuza during the murders, God would protect him. He was killed, standing in the doorway of his home.

Aunt Fanya, Naum's sister, had married a man in Moscow. She became pregnant and returned to Minsk to have her baby – a pretty little girl named Frieda. In the March slaughter, both Fanya and Frieda were killed. The parents of Joseph's sixteen-year-old cousins, Isia and Sarah, were killed. Isia went to work one day in a column and disappeared. Joseph learned later that Isia had escaped to the partisans, but unfortunately was captured by the Nazis and executed.

JOSEPH   The worst thing for me in the March 1942 onslaught is that Papa is missing. I have not seen or heard from him since the two of us joined separate columns on the second day of March.

For several days I look for him. I keep hoping I would find him. I am so close to him. Each day I ask persons in the factory and then at night back at the ghetto I inquire of neighbors if they have any word of Naum, my father.

It becomes difficult for me to speak to anyone. I cry so much about my beloved Papa's disappearance. Maybe he's alive, I think, and hiding somewhere. Maybe he has escaped and joined the partisans, and right now is helping to blow up German trains carrying troops and war stuff.

All my hopes are useless. An acquaintance who had been there, tells me the truth, the whole sad story. Papa had been marched, along with thousands of others, to the Ubileynaya Plaza, where he became a victim of a mass slaughter. They had shot Papa! Why? There was no reason, beyond his being a Jew.

Though it had been several days since father had been killed, I wandered over, anyway, to the Plaza, to view the hateful place. When I arrived I saw the results of yet another mass killing. Dead bodies were stacked like firewood for at least half a mile. The Gestapo had no time to have the graves and trenches on Zamkovaya Street dug fast enough for their appetites for blood.

I continue to wander around the Ubileynaya Plaza, and come upon a freshly covered trench, where thousands have just been buried. Suddenly, I see the vast hole move! And it keeps moving, in waves that are both wonderful and horrifying to me! I am still a mere child, but I quickly figure out that not everyone in the trench is dead. Many are wounded but still alive when the bulldozers pushed the dirt over them.

One such is Alek, a little boy like me, who had been in the hole. He had not been wounded; just shoved into the hole alive. Like a few others, he created an air-pocket inside his shirt and kept breathing. He pretended to be dead while the dirt poured over him, because German riflemen, he told me, walked alongside the pit, shooting anyone they saw move. When night fell, Alek climbed up over dozens of dead bodies and broke his way to the surface. We became good friends in the months ahead.

(After World War II, the people in Minsk collected money for a memorial to all their fellow men and women – between 7-8,000 of them – who had perished in the Ubileynaya Plaza. After it was built, the Soviet government would not allow anyone to pray or linger at the memorial. The KGB (secret police) kept close watch to make certain that no religious ceremonies were performed at either this or any other memorial in the Soviet Union).

True, two of Joseph's grandparents and many of his aunts, uncles, and cousins had been killed by the Germans and Byelorussians. But losing Naum, his beloved father, caused him to take the holocaust on a very personal basis.

JOSEPH   We moved to Suchaya Street. I don't know why we went there. It was for some reason or another that Mama picked the place. I didn't like it. It had no malena, and Mama wouldn't let me out on the street. She was afraid I would be picked up just like Papa and taken off somewhere and shot. So I just stayed home with Mama.

On one side of the house was the Jewish cemetery, and on the other side was the Russian territory where Byelorussians lived. One day Leva was playing with a hobbyhorse that grandfather Kiva made for him. A guy from the Russian territory climbed over the fence, threw Leva off the hobbyhorse and just took it to his side of the fence, leaving Leva behind, crying. The grown-ups came, but there was nothing that could be done.

By now the Minsk Jews had lost all trust in the German occupiers, and also in the Byelorussians who constantly abetted them. The idea for escape had been brewing in many people's minds, and a few did successfully get out, but now they collectively began to put their thoughts into action. As one of the first escape methods, the ghetto dwellers formed themselves into columns early each morning and walked outside just as though they were going to work in a German factory or some such thing. This ruse worked for three or four days until the Germans caught on. Regrettably, most of those who had left the ghetto in this manner were caught and severely punished, even with death: they simply had no place to go.

They could not expect help from people outside the ghetto. If a Russian citizen saw somebody who looked Jewish, or appeared to be wearing clothes from any kind of concentration camp, he called the police. To harbor an escaped Jew invited the death penalty. Making the Jews even more noticeable, they had to wear the yellow patch of the Star of David: if you didn't wear the Star of David, you could be killed on the spot.

The Germans continued their deliberate plans of terror. At one time they would eliminate this area in the ghetto and another time that area. Every night, after pumping up themselves with beer and schnapps, the Gestapo agents picked three to five houses into which to intrude. They didn't shoot anybody; they just cut their throats.

JOSEPH   One night the residents of a house near ours stayed awake, to try and guard themselves. It didn't help. They had no guns to resist these professional killers known as Nazis.

At our house Mama, Leva, grandfather Kiva, and I listen in horror to the screams of our neighbors, who, we know, are being slaughtered. No one sleeps in our home this night because we fear we will be the very next victims. In the early morning, things become quiet, and we know that the rampaging and killing has stopped, at least for now.

We get out very carefully in the morning, and the ground is red from the blood of at least fifty of our friends and neighbors. These are children, old men and women, and those not physically able to toil in the Nazi slave camps.

While we watch, again wondering how long we could personally endure before the Germans came for us, the Byelorussian police arrive. The weather was warming some, and the police announced that these bodies would have to dispensed within quick order. Otherwise, there would be a risk of epidemics, which would affect them as much as their Jewish victims. The police picked some men, handed out shovels, and ordered them to dig holes in which to bury the bodies.

Grandfather Kiva was one of those assigned to burial duty. He began to dig vigorously with me at his side, sifting through the dirt. Suddenly, Kiva's shovel connected with something solid, and thinking it was a stone, he dug more intensely. To empty his shovel, Kiva flung its contents away from him. Instead of a rock, something broke open and there was a shower of gold coins.

Grandfather and I had found a ceramic pot – around five gallons in capacity – full of gold coins that apparently had been buried at this place during the Revolution to keep them from falling into Communist hands. Before long everyone in the burial detail knew of the find and gleefully hovered around Kiva and me, hoping to get a part of the treasure. Suddenly an SS detail converged upon us and stopped the festivities. The Germans took all the gold, and made all of us shed our clothes and shake them out in the German presence to make sure no coins were being hidden.

What a coup this would have been! The gold was certainly worth much money, and it surely would have ameliorated some of the pain and suffering within the Minsk ghetto.

It was not until July that other widespread attacks occurred, so terribly that Jewish sobs "resounded through the streets, and gradually grew into one continuous wail. For the first time the people of the ghetto could not conceal their grief and pain."[19]

One of these happenings was very personal to Joseph Gavi: he came perilously close to losing Rachel, his mother.

JOSEPH   As if losing my father weren't enough, I come home one day – I don't remember from where – and find Mama missing.

I quickly learn from neighbors that Mama has been apprehended by the Germans – for what specific reason no one knew – and taken to the barn. I know what being in that barn means. I tear through the ghetto streets, and finally find a friend, one of my old music teachers, Greta Koffmann, who works at the Judenrat.

'Greta,' I gasped. 'Mama is in the barn! What can we do?'

'I will try to do something,' Greta responds.

I run away from her, not comforted by her promise to do something. I am so distressed that I didn't even want to be alive anymore. I finally go myself to the barn. A guard stands at the front door, armed with a machine gun.

I ask the guard to let me in. The guard, of course, knows what is going to happen to all the people inside the barn, and he refuses my entry. Then I start crying and I jump on the guard, hitting him with all my strength with my fists, and cursing him in German; the guard relents – he opens the door and shoves me inside.

I spend several minutes adjusting to the darkness, all the

---

[19] Ainsztein, Jewish Resistance, 479.

while loudly calling out Mama's name, Rachel. Mama finally recognizes my voice, and so we reunited. Thankfully, Leva had been left behind, at home with grandfather.

'What are you doing here?' Mama asked desperately, for she knew, just as the German guard had, what was going to happen to all these people crammed into the barn. I simply wanted to be with Mama at this point of crisis, and die with her if necessary. We thought we would be killed.

Mama and I embraced and waited for our executions. Suddenly, though, the door flew open, and the guard called out our names, 'Rachel and Joseph Gavi.'

They were let out. Greta Koffmann had talked to the right officials and saved their lives. The others in the barn that night were marched off a few minutes later and slaughtered in the nearby cemetery.

CHAPTER THREE

THE PARTISANS

B esides Greta Koffmann, another woman helped young Joseph fight the Nazis. Her name was Tzilia Khlebanov and she had been helping to plan Jewish escapes from the ghetto. In early spring 1943 Tzilia came for a group, but while getting them ready to move, she heard that the Germans had blocked off much of the partisan area – including the Naleboki Forest, where many of the Minsk Jews were taken. She could not move, so she had to stay in the ghetto until the Germans removed their blockade. While in the ghetto, Tzilia befriended Rachel and urged her to let Joseph become a guide. (He had stopped his daily march to the Voroshilov factory since Naum's death). His small stature, Tzilia told Rachel, made Joseph a perfect candidate for the job.

Tzilia told Joseph how to find the partisans. (The majority of people who escaped from the ghetto did not even know where to run, let alone how to find the partisans). She showed him which directions to take, how to avoid roaming Gestapo groups, and most importantly, she listed a few villages – Gaiche, Staroe Selo, and Medvezhino, for example – where the partisans had strongholds.

The partisans controlled some 150 square miles around Staroe Selo, Naleboki Forest, and Gaichi, an area full of thick bogs and swamps. "One could not drive through this territory," recalls Joseph, "not even the Germans," who knew that the partisans were there. In fact, the Germans fairly well had the partisans – which ultimately included many Poles as well as Russians – surrounded. But just as in the ghetto, ways were found to penetrate the lines so that people like Joseph could come and go almost at will.

Other young people besides Joseph helped Jews escape to the relative safety of the partisans. Bunya Hammer, thirteen years old, led more than a hundred out of the ghetto, as did his friend David Klenskiy. Twelve-year-old Tonya Zomer rescued some hundred people before the Germans caught and killed him. Four girls, Sima Peterson, Tonichka Gimpel, Rachel Pirklar, and Valya Rubenina, performed valiant work as well in the face of the Nazi tyranny. They were all short of stature, but not as short as Joseph.[20]

Only occasionally, when the Germans and Byelorussian policemen performed military operations like the blockade that stranded Tzilia in the Minsk ghetto, were the Germans an extreme threat to the partisans. Otherwise, the entire area was free to the point that the partisans could mobilize their members, both men and women, and collect food and other everyday necessities.

In time the partisans were even able to build a small landing strip from which several military and intelligence aircraft, primarily Y-2 airplanes, from Moscow and other unoccupied territories, given the general name, "Big Earth," could land and take off. On each of these occasions, news and orders were brought from the capital city, while gold, silver, other commodities, and ill or wounded partisans were sent back.

JOSEPH   Mama worried about me leaving and seeking the partisans. It was dangerous work for anyone, let alone a young boy, not yet twelve years old. But Mama knew, just as Papa had, that it was only a matter of time until the rest of our family would be killed. After all, the ghetto was shrinking daily, as German and Byelorussian thugs continued to shoot residents through the night and tighten up the fences by day, coming closer and closer to our house. Escaping to the partisans offered at least a chance for me to stay alive. Mama gave me her blessings.

On a spring day in 1943 I sneaked under a fence with no difficulty, and started walking. I pass Gaiche and come to Staroe Selo. The partisans spot me immediately as a newcomer, and are suspicious of me.

---

[20] Ainsztein, Jewish Resistance, 482.

"Where are you from? Who are you looking for? What are you looking for? Why are you here?" I tried to answer the questions that came so quickly to me. At first, no one would listen to me. For all the partisans know, I am a German spy, coming to find out their locations and report them to the authorities.

I am taken to a large barn (which, of itself, was frightening to me), on the outskirts of the village, where three guards keep me in confinement. By now I myself had some misgivings. Have I really found the partisans or are they police? Are they Nazi collaborators? Just where am I, anyway? Whoever they are, they keep me under heavy guard in this barn for about three days. Then they start questioning me again, and I repeated, "Khlebanov sent me. She is from the partisan group Kutuzov."

"How does she look?"

"She is somewhat short in body, and blonde in appearance."

"How does she talk?"

"Slowly."

They finally accepted me. They put me in a wagon and drove me to another village some thirty miles away in the Naleboki Forest. The partisans took me to headquarters where I was once again grilled with questions.

"How are the conditions in the concentration camp?"

"Terrible, and getting worse each day."

"How do you survive?"

"By cunning and good luck."

Yes, the partisan leaders told me, we believe you.

After giving me more food that I had had in months, they instructed me to go back to the ghetto and get Tzilia and bring her back with me.

Everyone in the ghetto was ecstatic to see me again. I had been away less than a week, but under the circumstances it had seemed an eternity. I told Tzilia that the partisans wanted to see her, so the two of us prepared for the trip ahead. We slipped under the fence in the early hours of the morning. I was first because of my size, and Tzilia next. I kept a careful eye out for German guards.

We walked through the day and finally got back to Staroe Selo, where we were met by a group of partisans. After supper, Tzilia and I, both tired from our day's march, went to a nearby barn where there was dry hay, to sleep through the night. I fell asleep immediately, but some time later I was awakened by fierce movements and crying.

Someone was saying urgently, "Don't do this. Please don't do this."

Tzilia was being raped by a partisan named Vishnevski. I was just a small boy and I had never known of anything like this before. I did not know what was going on. It was only later, after seeing many more things like this, that I began to understand.

Later in the year, 1943, the partisan leadership found that Vishnevski had a pattern of misdeeds. He would go into villages and take money and other valuables from citizens, all in the name of Mother Russia, and then spend it all on himself. There was also a pattern of rape and other crimes against innocent villagers. He was tried by the partisans, convicted, and sentenced to death by firing squad. Apparently, Vishnevski was so hated by everyone that about 500 people gathered for his execution, which occurred late at night in early December. Tzilia was there, though she never told anybody why. Joseph knew why, but the two never even mentioned the rape in the barn.

Among the partisan groups, one was named "family." Because the Russian partisans would not readily accept all the Jews who escaped from the ghetto, one escapee, Shlomo Zoring, organized a group of old men and women and young children who, somehow and miraculously, had so far escaped the Nazi yoke. His group was the seventh unit of the Katuzov Detachment, commanded by Israel Lapidus, and it was known as the 106th Detachment. Showing their general unfriendliness to all Jewish escapees, the partisans routinely relieved them of their guns, shoes, money, gold, and any other valuables they might have. After taking everything of value from them, they handed them over to Zoring, who led them to the family partisans who operated deep in the Naleboki Forest. There they lived in relative peace and quiet, until Liberation Day on July 3, 1944.

Perhaps some of this "peace and quiet" was due to Zoring's family partisans building imitation guns out of wood. They looked exactly like big guns, aimed in the direction from which the Germans would attack if they ever decided to do so. Zoring's group and another one led by A. Belsky went from one village to another begging the residents for food, and they usually got just enough to stay alive.

Tzilia and Joseph belonged to the militant partisans. Their job was to kill Nazis, fight the police and collaborators, and attack German military forces, by planting explosive devices at bridges and railroads they knew the enemy would be using.

JOSEPH   From Staroe Selo, I was appointed as a messenger and leader of escapees from the Minsk ghetto. Each week I slipped back into the ghetto, but not to my home on Suchaya Street. In fact, Mama never even knew the times I had returned. The partisans feared that if I was ever able to lead Mama and Leva out, I would quit working for them. This was certainly not true; nevertheless, I am sure it was a very real problem for those working against the Nazi horrors.

In the ghetto each week I was taken to a house on Flaksa Street, where the Jewish Underground operated. They hid me there, fed me well, and I stayed for two or three days until an escapee group could be put together. Generally, each group was composed of fifteen to twenty members. There were women, men, boys like me, and girls in the groups I led away from the ghetto.

Their escapes did not come free of charge. Those chosen every week or so to be led out of the ghetto by Joseph had to turn in some of their material possessions to the Underground. This way, the partisans, Jews and others, usually received a bit of gold, diamonds, watches, typewriters, radios, and every now and then a few guns. Once these were delivered to the partisans at Staroe Selo, they were then sent to the central government in Moscow to be sold for money with which to build tanks and other war machines.

JOSEPH   From the spring of 1943 to the time the ghetto was closed in late 1943 I go back and forth between the partisans in Staroe Selo and the Minsk ghetto at least a dozen times, and altogether lead over 200 people to safety. My duties, however, were mixed.

Sometimes Joseph was sent to Minsk, not to conduct groups trying to escape, but to bring and take messages between the partisans and the Minsk ghetto Underground. One riveting experience he had was to try to bring a large quantity – some 150 kilograms – of much needed medicine of different kinds from Minsk to Gaiche, Staroe Selo, and other villages occupied by the partisans.

Where the medicines came from was anybody's guess. In all likelihood, they had been secreted out of various hospitals and hidden by the Underground until they could be delivered to the partisans. No matter. The medicines were now in the Minsk ghetto, and with a little bit of effort and good luck they could be gotten to those who needed them most: the Russian partisans.

The Underground found two construction workers who had been impressed by the Germans into service as wagon drivers. Thus, they would know of any significant event such as the shipment of a large supply of medicine. Joseph's job was to find these two men, and lead them to the partisans.

JOSEPH   I slipped through the ghetto fence, walked a block or two, and found a horse-drawn wagon, prearranged by the Underground. I drove the wagon to the construction site, where the two men waited for me with the medicines. Quickly they loaded the medicines and, with me on the front seat, headed out of town for Staroe Selo. The two shouted, "Let's go!" But before we were even out of town, the two construction workers got cold feet. They were scared, and wanted to go back.

"Why go back?" I incredulously asked. "We have a fortune here, with all this medicine. Not even Russian civilians have this kind of medicine, let alone the Jews in the ghetto and the partisans in the woods. Why, then, should we go back?"

Certainly, if we were caught, the consequences would be grave. No amount of my persuading could induce them to continue. Out of fear of the terror that awaited them if we were apprehended, the two men took the medicines away from me, and turned back. No amount of money, they apparently believed, was worth the risk they were taking.

I returned to the Underground house on Flaksa Street, and told the leaders everything that had happened. During the night the Underground commanders found the two wagon drivers, who had hidden the medicines. The commanders talked them into trying again next day, in the name of patriotism and monetary gain. They were told not to look nervous, but to appear as though they had all the self-confidence in the world. They would hold onto their medicines as I led the wagon toward Staroe Selo.

I had already decided that if the drivers refused to cooperate this time, I would go back to the partisans and not return to the ghetto. I didn't want to stay around here and die for nothing.

Early next morning I slipped through a fence and went to the construction site where the two Jewish construction workers/ drivers awaited me. Luckily, it was raining, sometimes heavily, and it was logical for the drivers to cover up their faces, to keep the rain off, but important, too, as disguises. Certainly, the first SS man or Byelorussian police to recognize us as Jewish would kill us on the spot.

Just outside the city limits, we turned in a western direction, and after a few miles our worst fears materialized. Coming in the opposite direction were ten to fifteen horse wagons, each one filled with Byelorussian policemen! Each policeman wore a black uniform and on each shoulder was the hateful swastika. My comrades and I thought our time had come.

We pulled off the side of the road to let the police procession, hopefully, go by. It took two or three of the longest minutes I can remember before they passed on by. We were so scared; we thought it was the end.

On the first question, everything would be lost: the Jewish drivers, the wagon, the horses, I, and above everything else, the medicines which were so vital to the continuance of the partisan movement. But it was raining heavily. The policemen kept their eyes straight on the road ahead, and they, too, were heavily cloaked against the elements. Thank God they didn't stop us, because it was raining so heavily. If it hadn't been for the rain, surely they would have stopped us. I have liked rain ever since.

He and the two drivers were heroes when they arrived at Staroe Selo. (After the war, Joseph was much decorated by the Soviet government for his services to the Mother Country). There were many celebrations in honor of their safe return with such a valuable load of medicines. Music, food, and many rounds of the samogon ("moonshine") bottle accompanied the festivities.

Another part of Joseph's duties was to make contact with units that had been drafted into the German army. He was sent one time to contact a group of forty-five Slovakians who, though wearing German uniforms, wanted to fight against them. These men were from Yugoslavia and Czechoslovakia and hated the Germans for their imperialism and hateful ways. Joseph led them back to the partisans at Staroe Selo, where they were gratefully welcomed.

Like everything else in the Soviet Union, the partisan groups in Staroe Selo and surrounding territories, for some inexplicable reason, were ordered by Moscow to move to a different location. Good enough, but for Joseph it was a problem; the new place was seventy-five miles from Minsk, and obviously he could not return to the ghetto every week. For that matter, he doubted that he would ever get back to Minsk.

JOSEPH My commander told me to get Mama and Leva and bring them out of Minsk once and for all. I slipped back into the ghetto as I had done so many times before and went straightway to the Underground house on Flaksa Street. The Underground had already begun to form the next group that I would lead out. I insisted that they get Mama and Leva and have them join this group. It had been more than three months since I had seen them, and three months under the circumstances was a very long time. We embraced in tears when Mama walked into the Underground headquarters. I missed Mama; after all, I was still a little boy of twelve.

Problems developed. The group that had been put together for escape would not agree to the idea of taking Leva along. He was an infant, and a cry in the night caused by fear or hunger would bring the authorities down upon us. Even Mama could not guarantee that Leva would stay quiet. For a time it appeared that Mama would not go with me, because she did not want to leave Leva behind.

I finally resolved the difficulty by promising Mama that if she came with me and the group, I would return immediately and bring out Leva. This mollified Mama, so Leva was left in the ghetto with a friend and grandfather Kiva. The group, which now included my beloved mother, waited for a dark, moonless night, and so began our escape.

Joseph cut the wires of a fence and had each of the group (some fifteen of them altogether) crawl underneath on his or her belly. The first obstacle to any escape was a nearby railroad track. It had been fitted with semaphoric signals to go off in noise and lights if anyone touched it at night. Joseph carefully explained to everyone why they should not touch the railroad track.

Slowly, slowly, and ever so meticulously, the group passed over the track. And it almost worked! One of the last escapees, nervous, terrified, and trying to crawl on his stomach across a railroad track without touching it, succumbed to his frustrations.

Everywhere around them noise, but for some reason, no lights, exploded, and the furious voices of German guards were heard coming toward them. The escaping group began to panic, and everyone ran off in all directions. They found ditches and small houses and sheds to hide behind. Joseph and Rachel stayed together and carefully sidled away from the railroad track. Every few minutes they stopped, listening for the police they knew to be so near. Besides worrying about himself and Rachel, Joseph also wondered how he could ever get this group – whatever was left of it – back together. It was so dark that he could not see any of them.

Fortunately, the darkness also kept the Germans from seeing them. The place finally became quiet and the Germans apparently believed the semaphore system had malfunctioned, so they went back to their guardhouses.

Miraculously, none of the group was a Nazi casualty that night. Everyone came together in about an hour, a distance now between them and the railroad, and started anew for Staroe Selo. With all the twisting and turning in the darkness, however, Joseph himself had become lost. The best thing he knew to do was walk – just walk – and hope it would be in the right direction.

JOSEPH   After walking for some time, I see a large light projector and order my followers to the ground. Immediately, I see that we are facing from a distance a prison camp of some sort, because the light comes from a squarely built structure that I know all too well as a guardpost.

There is a large potato field between us refugees and the guardpost. I order them all to lie down in the rows of the green potato field, whose plants had grown tall. The searchlights come around at intervals but do not spot us or the small amounts of luggage I had allowed them to bring.

As soon as daylight arrives, I order the group to stay put in the potato field and, since I am the leader and the shortest among us, I slide out to try and determine our location. All day I spend slinking around the place where the concentration camp is located, approaching peoples' houses and asking for help. At the end of my queries, I know the way to Staroe Selo: it is between six and seven kilometers away. I slip back into the potato field in the afternoon to inform Mama and my followers of what I had found.

But my group could not travel in the daytime, for we surely would be spotted by the Germans. I join Mama and the rest of the group who had been lying quiet and still in the potato field. They certainly cannot stand up during this cruel ordeal, or eat, or talk except in whispers, or even make a pee. They cannot do anything. Mama and the group now appreciate the decision to leave Leva behind.

At dawn Joseph stealthily led his group out of the potato patch. Several hours later, they approached the village of Medvezhino. All of a sudden they heard shouts of "Halt! HALT!" and shooting began and bullets whizzed by them. As one, they hit the ground, and expected to be killed within a matter of minutes. "It's a strange feeling," Joseph says, lying on the ground hearing "bullets fly around like bees," waiting for the Germans or Byelorussians to find you. Many in the group, fearing that the end had come, began sobbing and lamenting aloud. Fortunately for Joseph's group, but tragically for someone else, the police passed them by. They never knew why, and did not worry about it.

The group waited for another several hours and then began to move again. Wearily they made their way, and by noon were in Staroe Selo, tired and hungry but elated that they had found their way to the partisans. They lauded Joseph for his leadership skills, and for his courage in the face of mortal danger.

Joseph, though, did not stay in Staroe Selo very long. He told the authorities that his two-year-old brother was back in Minsk and that he had solemnly promised his mother that he would go back and get him. And so he did, but not without some troublesome moments along the way. He arrived back in Minsk in mid-afternoon and had to wait in hiding until nightfall before re-entering the ghetto. Inside, he found Leva and a teenage girl, who had been looking after him.

JOSEPH The three of us started out. I carried Leva until I was completely exhausted. I had not slept for the past three days. The girl relieved me of my burden, making things a bit easier, at least for a while. I was concerned, too, because grandfather Kiva had refused to come because his legs were so swollen that he could not walk.

But then an extremely heavy rain comes down. We are in a forest, and again – because of the weather and fatigue – I become disoriented. There is no point in trying to continue forward in such a storm, so I decide to protect Leva from the rain as best I can. The three of us lie down in the forest, and I lay on top of Leva to protect him from the rain.

I immediately fall asleep because I have been going now for more than three days without any rest. I sleep soundly and, as I thought, so did Leva, because there is not a sound from my little brother. When I awake several hours later, however, I look at Leva in horror. Leva is blue! He has not been able to breathe freely with my body over him. He is near death. Frantically, the girl and I work on Leva's little body with artificial respiration until we see some signs of life. Everything is all right! Leva laboriously starts to breathe, causing me, in nervous tension and elation, to break into tears of joy.

The three of us soon came to a village. The people there were good. They gave us something to eat. They knew what we were trying to do, and they didn't ask about it. The less spoken, the better. After the food, the villagers gave me, Leva, and Leva's caretaker directions on how to avoid the Germans and the Byelorussian police, who were thick in the area.

The partisans at Staroe Selo – who thought something had gone wrong – were just about to depart when my two traveling companions and I showed up. I kept my promise! I kept my promise! I shouted out, and Mama was so happy to have her two sons restored to her.

But then, Mama, Leva, and the girl were taken to Zoring's family partisan group. Before departure, the partisans lined up everyone and confiscated any weapons (taken, generally, from dead and captured Germans) and jewelry they might have in their possession. In this way, Joseph lost the Kirov factory handmade watch that Leva's baby-sitter had given him for helping save her life.

Joseph himself was spirited off right away to the fighting partisans. As they walked deeper and deeper into the dense Soviet forests, Joseph tearfully wondered how long it would be before he saw Leva and his beloved mother again. As it turned out, it was about a year, late 1944, before he was rejoined with the part of his family that still existed.

After marching several days Joseph's group of partisans halted, and soon Joseph found out that they were near the Soviet city of Baranovichi. There was an airstrip in their new location, and frequently the Soviet authorities in Moscow sent instructions to the partisans about where the Germans were, and who were the Nazi collaborators in the area.

JOSEPH   One of my first assignments was to Baranovichi itself to do intelligence work on a collaborator – this one, a newspaper editor who had begun to cooperate with the Nazi invaders, and who had damaged the Soviet cause by his pro-German editorials. The editor was under a death sentence by the Kremlin officials and my group of partisans was ordered to carry it out.

I am commanded to find out certain things about this newspaper editor. Where does he live? How many floors up? What time does he go to work? Does he walk to work? Or does he go by horse-wagon, or auto? Who lives with him. Is he guarded by anyone?

I dress in dirty beggar's clothes and head for Baranovichi. As a beggar, I travel from street to street in the wealthy section of town, beseeching people to provide me with food. I believe in this way that I will ultimately be led to the editor's home.

Only when I discover where the newspaper is located, however, do I find my quarry. I wait outside the newspaper office and then secretly follow the editor home. I watched the newspaper man's home for three days, each night going to a nearby railroad station, where I sleep in one of the boxcars located there.

On the fourth day I bolster up my courage and go directly to the man's front door and ring the bell. The editor, himself, answers.

"I want some bread," I told him.

The man goes away and returns moments later with a couple of pieces of bread in his hand, which he gives me.

"Thank you," I say simply, nibbling on the bread and turning quickly away and running down the street.

Pre-war Minsk. Sovetskaya Street, 1939.

Pre-war Minsk. Sportsmen's parade on Lenin Square, 1939.

Minsk. Area of the Minsk ghetto, 1944

*Forcing Jews into the
Minsk ghetto, 1941.
(Minsk Museum,
Belarus.)*

The Minsk Jewish ghetto during the German occupation, 1941-1944. The sign in German means "Warning: Those who pass this fence will be shot." (Minsk Museum, Belarus.)

Upper left: Young Joseph Gavi, 15 years old, left, just after release from Soviet navy.

Upper Right: Ida standing on the slopes of Mount Elbrus, highest point in Europe.

Right: 1936: Uncle Isaac, his son, Joseph, and Isaac's wife.

ЗАГАД

НА ЎТВАРЭНЬНЕ ЖЫДОЎСКАГА ЖЫЛОГА РАЁНУ Ў г. МЕНСКУ

1.

Пачынаючы ад даты гэтага загаду, у горадзе Менску будзе вылучана асобная частка гораду выключна на пражываньне жыдоў.

2.

Усё жыдоўскае жыхарства гораду Менску абавязана пасьля агалошаньня гэтага загаду на працягу 5-цёх дзён перабрацца ў жыдоўскі раён. Калі хто з жыдоў пасьля сканчэньня гэтага тэрміну будзе знойдзены ня ў гэтым жыдоўскім раёне, ён будзе арыштаваны і як найстражэй пакараны. Няжыдоўскае жыхарства, што жыве ў межах жыдоўскага жылога раёну, мае безадкладнейшым чынам пакінуць жыдоўскі раён. Калі вызваленых жыдамі памешканьняў на ў жыдоўскім раёне не акажацца, Аддзел Прыдзелу Памешканьняў Менскай Гарадзкой Управы адвядзе іншыя вольныя памешканьні.

3.

Дапушчаецца браць з сабою хатнюю маемасьць. Хто будзе зьлоўлены на забіраньні чужога дабра або рабаваньні, будзе карацца праз расстрэл.

4.

Жыдоўскі раён абмяжоўваецца наступнымі вуліцамі: Калгасны завулак з прылягальнем Калгаснай вуліцы, далей паўз рэчку з прылягальнем Ніжняй вуліцы, выключаючы праваслаўную царкву, з прыляг. да Рэспубліканскай вуліцы, з прылягальнем Шорнай вул., Калектарнай вуліцы, Мэбальнага завулку, Перакопскай вуліцы, Нізавой вуліцы, Жылоўскіх могілак, Абуткавой вуліцы, Другога Апанскага завулку, Заслаўскай вуліцы аж да Калгаснага завулка.

5.

Жыдоўскі жылы раён мае быць зараз-жа пасьля сканчэньня перабараў агароджаны каменным мурам ад рэшты гораду. Мураваньне гэтага муру мусіць быць зроблена жыхарамі жыдоўскага раёну, прычым за будаўляны матар'ял будзе ісьці каменьне з нежылых або зруінаваных будынкаў.

6.

Бытаваньне ня ў жылым жыдоўскім раёне жыдоў, зграмаджаным у рабочыя жыдоўскія дружыны, ёсьць забаронена. Гэтыя дружыны могуць высьці са свайго раёну толькі маючы накіраваньне на пэўныя месцы працы, вызначаныя Менскай Гарадзкой Управай. Парушэньні гэтага загаду будуць карацца праз расстрэл.

7.

Жыдам дазволена ўлаходзіць і выходзіць з жыдоўскага раёну толькі дзьвюма вуліцамі: Апанскай і Астроўскай. Пералазіць праз мур забараняецца. Нямецкая варта і варце службы парадку загадана страляць у парушальнікаў гэтага.

8.

У жыдоўскі жылы раён могуць уваходзіць адны толькі жыды і асобы якія належаць да нямецкіх вайсковых фармаваньняў і да Гарадзкой Менскай Управы і толькі на выпадак справы.

9.

[...] жыдоўскую раду [...] пазіка 30.000 чырвонцаў на ўзнаўленьне [...] перабарамі. Гэтыя грошы, працэнтная аплата якіх [...] будзе ўстаноўлена, [...] быць зложаны на працягу 12 гадзін пасьля выданьня гэтага загаду ў касу [...] Управы (будынак па вул. Маркса, 28).

10.

Жыдоўская [...] рада зараз-жа павінна даць Аддзелу прыдзелу памешканьняў Гарадзкой Управы заяву пра ўсе жыдамі пакінутыя памешканьні, якія знаходзяцца ня ў жыдоўскім раёне і ашчэ не занятыя арыйскім (няжыдоўскім) жыхарствам.

11.

Парадак у жыдоўскім жылым раёне будуць трымаць асобныя жыдоўскія дружыны парадку (адмысловы загад на гэта будзе сваім часам).

12.

За канчатковыя перабары жыдоўскіх жыхароў у іхні раён поўную адказнасьць мае Жыдоўская Рада гораду Менску. Усялякія парушэньні гэтага загаду будуць як найстражэй пакараны.

ПАЛЁВЫ КАМЭНДАНТ

Выдавец—Выдавецтва „Менск". · Друкарня

German order for Jews to move to certain parts of the ghetto. Names of the streets in the ghetto, and punishment for people who do not follow orders.

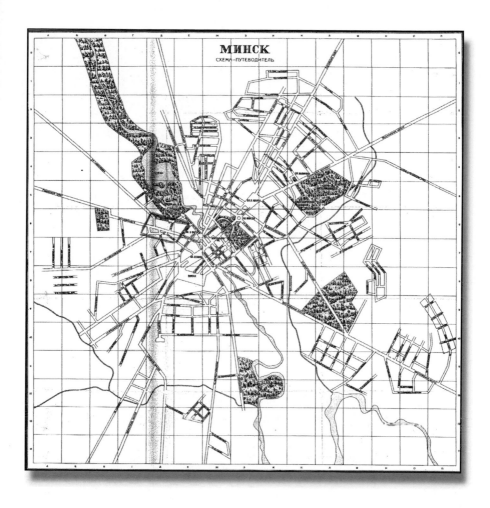

Minsk, 1939. 1-2 pogrom–November 7 and 20, 1941. 3-4 pogrom–March 2 and 31, 1942. 5 pogrom–October 21, 1943.

Destroyed Minsk. Nemiga Street, 1940s.

Minsk destroyed by Germans.

Destroyed Minsk. Lenin Street.

Destroyed during war Minsk. Intersection of Sovetskaya and Lenin streets.

„В военном деле, а тем более в такой войне, как современная война, нельзя стоять на месте. Остановиться в военном деле— значит отстать." И. СТАЛИН.

УЧЕБНЫЙ ОТРЯД КРАСНОЗНАМЕННОГО БАЛТИЙСКОГО ФЛОТА

ОБЪЕДИНЕННАЯ ШКОЛА

ГРАМОТА

Товарищу к/фл *Гави*

Иосифу Семеновичу

За отличное окончание

Объединенной школы

объявляю благодарность

и награждаю грамотой

Начальник школы
капитан 2 ранга *Вашанур* (ШАКЛЕЦОВ)

Приказ по Объединенной школе
№ *143* от *14.06* 1945 г.

гор. Ораниенбаум

Medal for partisan activities during the war with Zhukov Division.

I rush back to the partisan group and tell my commander what I have seen and heard. A few days later, the newspaper editor is killed.

As early as 1943 the partisan groups operating in dense forests near big Russian cities which had been occupied by the Germans started a draft system. All able-bodied village men twenty years and up were conscripted into service for the partisans. They had no choice: whether they liked it or not, they joined the partisans. And if they adamantly refused, there could always be the bullet to the head. In some instances, villagers became as opposed to the partisans as to the Germans. It was not all that unusual for partisans to walk into a village on one end of a street while villagers ran to the other end of the street to warn the German that "partisans are coming."

The partisans, all with their headquarters deep in the Russian forests, were divided into three groups. The first were the terrorists who blew up railroad and telephone lines, trains and electrical stations, and planted land mines on highways so German patrols would be in mortal danger. Second were the attack groups who frequently surprised German troops who had taken over a village. And, finally, there were the foraging groups whose job was to keep the other two groups as well fed as humanly possible. This group traveled from village to village gathering hogs, even dogs, potatoes, bread, and guns whenever they were available.

One time the supply group went so deep inside a forest that the village people had never seen an airport or even a railroad. The partisans asked for food and supplies, but the villagers refused them. One of the partisans took out a compass. Then he asked, as Joseph heard the story, a house-owner: "Do you see how this thing moves?"

"Yes I do," said the entranced property holder. "What is it?"

"It is a device that perhaps will make you cooperate with us."

"How is that?"

"It is a compass and it will show us where you are hiding the food and other supplies, and when it does, we will take everything. If you cooperate with us now, however, and show us some goodwill, we will take only what we need."

The partisans got everything they wanted.

The foraging groups would take what they had collected – vegetables and meat – back to their camp where the cook made up everything into stews, using a big pot. Salt was scarce to non-existent, but the partisans did not stay hungry for long. The camp even constructed its own bakery, making bread from flour seized from the villages. These activities, of course, caused many villagers to resent the partisans. Sometimes when the partisans entered an area, one of its residents would sneak to the other end of the village to warn any Germans present that, "the Partisans have arrived," giving the Germans a chance to escape partisan wrath.

Joseph was not quite sure where his partisan group was located, except that it was somewhere in a forest in the vicinity of Baranovichi. The foraging groups brought mostly whole cows and whole hogs that had been butchered in the villages from whence they came. The partisans cut up these animals and cooked them just a little on open fires, and then hung the pieces of meat on trees, where the cool weather kept them from spoiling. Every time someone got hungry, they simply untied some beef or pork – or occasionally chicken (the villagers knowing that their food supplies were at risk both from Germans and Russian partisans, ate their pullets and roosters first) – from a tree and cooked it. "So in this way," Joseph remembers, "the partisans were not starving."

JOSEPH When my commander gave me a new assignment I was thrilled, for it put me right at the heart of partisan intelligence work. I was sent to a group of partisan 'terrorists' whose mission was to blow up railroad tracks. My job was to spend entire days hiding in the brush around the railroad track clocking appearances of German patrols, hoping to establish a pattern so that I could accurately report the number of minutes that would pass before the Germans returned. After a few days, I established such a pattern.

I go back to the partisans and lead a group to the railroad track where they successfully plant big blocks of TNT before the next train's arrival. They blow up the tracks, much to my satisfaction.

Within the partisan group, which must have numbered some 1,000 men and women, a special unit made explosives. They find unexploded Red Army bombs in the woods. I help the partisans to put the heads of the unexploded bombs into a large pot of boiling water. When the heads are melted they are poured into specially fabricated forms encased in black powder. These were the explosive bricks. We made hundreds of these, and placed them every five or ten meters around various areas of Byelorussian railroad tracks – -literally dozens of miles. The partisans dubbed these activities the 'railroad war,' and it was devastating.

Since I had reconnoitered in many of the areas where railroad tracks were located, my job was to guide the explosives groups to their desired destinations. They mainly wanted to blow up tracks, but what if a train should happen along? Especially a troop train?

Actually, the partisans hoped they would not encounter German trains. Each of these trains was generally outfitted with heavy arms, and machine guns could wreak havoc on a partisan group trying to blow up a track. If the partisans tried to escape, many of these trains were outfitted with artillery. So the partisans tried simply to blow up the tracks and not directly confront the German trains.

And what of the Germans during all these activities? What were they doing? They tried, of course, to stop these actions against them. But what could they do, being victims of so many hit and run tactics? The partisans would blow up a railroad and then, led by Joseph Gavi, disappear into the dense Soviet woods. For the most part, the Germans could not call for help or reinforcements. Most of their comrades were at the front; besides, downed telephone and electricity lines made communications next to impossible. Joseph relished the thought of being in a group that made German lives increasingly miserable.

Could the Germans have penetrated the forests and found the partisans? Perhaps so, but it would have taken herculean efforts and time that they did not have.

The partisans dug holes some seven feet deep in the forest, wide enough for two to four people to fit into. The last person in each night pulled a big piece of wood over the hole and, as best he could, scattered tree branches and other foliage over it. This was a "zemlanka," and apparently it worked very well. The camouflage was so effective that the partisans were never really afraid of being found in the forests.

Sometimes the partisans and the Germans came face to face without any violence between them. One such time was in the early winter of 1944. By orders from Moscow the partisans around Baranovichi were instructed to move to another location where their effectiveness of blowing up tracks and knocking out communications would be enhanced.

It snowed heavily and because they had to carry so many things – machine guns, blankets, clothing, bullets, shells, and other materials – they could not move very quickly. This was especially so in all the drifts, which sometimes went up over a man's shoulders. Most of their horse wagons were without wheels, so they used sleds, not for transporting people, but to carry fighting materials and clothes. Everybody within Joseph's unit had to walk – with one significant exception: Joseph Gavi himself. If Joseph had had to walk, he would never have made it, he was so short. He sat back and savored the comfort of the sled, pulled by a trusty horse.

Partisan scouts discovered a train at Negoreloe full of German soldiers. Accordingly, the partisans diverted their march some twelve miles west of the village, where the railroad crossing was guarded by some 500 Germans in bunkers along the track. Before arriving at these bunkers, some of the partisans had slipped through and cut telephone lines, so there was no chance for the Nazis in the bunkers to contact the trainload of their compatriots back at Negoreloe.

The partisan brigades, numbering about 1,000 men, were ready to destroy the German bunkers if there was any semblance of interference with their movements. Witnessing such a large group of Russians, the Germans evidently decided not to start a fight – even though the Germans were outnumbered here two to one, their firepower was superior to anything the Russian partisans had – so the partisans crossed the railroad without incident, in full view of the Germans. Even so, "we were very scared." This "standoff" near Negoreloe was one of the few occasions in World War II in Russia where a confrontation ended happily.

When the partisans got about six kilometers from the point of crossing the railroad track, apparently the military train from Negoreloe arrived, and the Germans then did start firing – supposedly to impress their commanders in their reports – but too late, for all the partisans were well out of range. The firing was more symbolic than real.

By noon the partisans were in thick forest and marshes, where the Germans were reluctant to follow. Coming to a village, the partisans took over different houses and huts.

JOSEPH I end up in a house where the kindly hostess feeds me scrambled eggs with fried lard, blintzes and honey, washed down by herbal tea. I become so comfortable here that thoughts of war quickly recede from my mind.

The middle of the next day the partisans arrived at their new location. The weather was still so bad that no anti-German activities could be carried out. They had no tents, and the ground was too frozen to dig zemlankas. Fortunately, the local villagers were friendly to the partisans and agreed to put them up in their homes. Unbelievably, along with their owners, some twenty to twenty-five partisans were lodged in each house of several villages. And they stayed for about two and a half months – until spring arrived. When the weather warmed up, the partisans – again with Joseph as one of their guides – went after the Germans. They knew it was a two-way street – every man of them knew that the Germans would soon be coming after them.

In July 1944, the day arrived that Joseph and his partisan colleagues had been waiting for: liberation! Their day of deliverance was at hand.

But it was not at all the joyous occasion Joseph had expected. First, Josef Stalin was reluctant to accept as heroes many of the Jewish groups who had escaped from ghettoes and joined partisan groups. (Nevertheless, Joseph Gavi certainly did receive his share of Soviet honors, in the form of medals from the Army, for his work in leading people out of the Minsk ghetto and then guiding the fighting partisans to railroad and electrical and telephone facilities, so they could be blown up. Undoubtedly, he would have been awarded additional medals if he hadn't been a Jew).

Second, there was a problem with a large group of the partisans who came, not from Russia, but from Poland. The partisan activities in the Naleboki forests were close to Polish territory. While the war was in progress, a Polish government in exile established itself in Oxford, England, and directed many activities of the Polish Underground against the German occupiers. Moreover, many of the Polish partisans were in the Minsk area and became quite popular with the local residents.

Perhaps it was this popularity that worried the Soviet government so much. With the Polish government-in-exile being overly exposed to western ideas, and the partisan Poles expected to be included in the first round of Russian military liberation from the Germans, Stalin had several real fits of paranoia. (After all, in 1940, he had ordered the unspeakable massacre of 1,500 Polish intellectuals in the Katyn Forest).

Thus he decided, well before the Germans were out of Russia, to neutralize all of the Polish partisans. He ordered that every man and woman of them be dismissed – immediately. Why? Because he was afraid they would turn their guns against the Russians themselves? Probably.

The Poles knew nothing of Stalin's secret order to disarm them, and deprive them of the means to fight against the Germans in the final days of World War II. Obeying Stalin's orders, the Russian partisans surrounded the Polish partisan groups and ordered them to surrender their arms. The Poles were outraged; they felt betrayed. They had fought as long and as bravely as the Russian partisans, yet here they were being treated as though they were the enemy. At that point in Soviet history, from Stalin's point of view, they were.

There was outrage. There was defiance, only to be met by the overwhelming force of the Russian partisans. Then there was obedience. And then there was reaction. After all the Polish guns had been laid to rest, an uncommonly large proportion of the Polish partisans engaged in miserable fistfights with their Russian (not German this time) tormentors. But Stalin had his way on this, as well as on so many other matters. The Poles were quickly and cruelly subordinated to the Soviet system.

The first order that came from the Russian government when it "united" the partisans was that every person, man and woman, between eighteen and fifty join the regulars. Each brigade of the partisans was ordered to march its troops to certain locations and turn their charges over to the regular Russian army.

JOSEPH   My group was headed by Ivan Vasilievich Yakubovski, who became a Captain in the Red Army at the ending of the war. At the beginning of the war, he had been captured by the Germans. After a short confinement, he escaped, and joined the Russian partisans in Naleboki Forest. Soon after the partisan movement began to shape into an organized form, he became a commander of the Kutuzov camp of the Zhukov Brigade of partisans.

Yakubovski took a liking to me, and in fact, wanted to adopt me as his son. 'If we are not going to find your mother' (who with Leva was still with Zoring's group) he said, 'I want to be your father.'

I was thirteen years old and I traveled around with Captain Yakubovski to Baranovichi in the immediate postwar period. He was good to me. He was just like a father. The weather was so warm and dry that for a week in Baranovichi my comrades and I slept under the open skies without tents.

Together, Joseph and Yakubovski went to Volkovish, in Poland, to find refugees there and tell them they were liberated, and that sustenance was on the way. The Poles in this camp slept outside, the weather was still so warm in July 1944, waiting for the Russian authorities to give them instructions on how to return to their homes and jobs. The Russians were in a hurry; they wanted to tell the inhabitants of Volkovisk, and indeed other villagers, what to do before the Polish government-in-exile could get in touch with them.

Joseph and Yakubovski, however, were invited by a local Catholic priest to stay in his house, an offer they gratefully accepted. The priest gave them ample portions of food and drink, and then put the two together to sleep in his guest room.

Once inside the special guest room, Yakubovski and Joseph began to relax.

JOSEPH   Suddenly, Yakubovski pointed to a window ledge.

"Look Joseph," he said. "What do you see on the window ledge?"

"Yes, I see it," I replied. "It's a watch."

"Take it," ordered Yakubovski.

"Why? I don't understand," I replied.

"Just take it," the Russian officer ordered again.

I take it. And then fall sound asleep until early the next morning. We two arose at dawn and immediately walk toward the village – some three to five miles – where the Polish refugees are located. Only minutes into our journey, a jeep came to a screeching halt beside us. It was full of Russian soldiers, an officer and the priest, who had offered his hospitality to us the night before.

"Where is the watch?" asked the priest. "Who took it?" pointing an accusing finger at me.

"Yes, I took the watch," I remarked, in a forlorn manner. I took the watch out of my pocket and handed it to the priest. But one of the officers was not satisfied. "Now" he ordered, "take off your pants."

Joseph did so, and the officer, taking off his belt, punished thirteen-year-old Joseph Gavi with a dozen lashes for taking a property that he had been put up to take in the first place. Joseph refused to implicate Yakubovski, because he knew that as an adult and a military officer in wartime Russia, he could very well get the death penalty, even for petty theft. Nevertheless, Joseph Gavi was reinforced in a lesson he already knew, and painfully at that: he alone was responsible for his actions, and he was actually to trust no one in this world, not even his closest acquaintances.

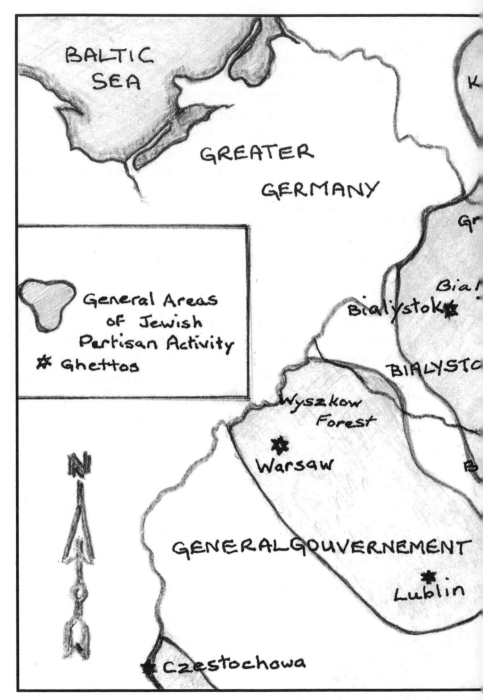

BALTIC SEA

GREATER GERMANY

K

Gr

General Areas of Jewish Partisan Activity
✴ Ghettos

Bia!

Bialystok✴

BIALYSTO

N

Wyszkow Forest

✴
Warsaw

B

GENERAL GOUVERNEMENT

✴ Lublin

✴ Czestochowa

Map indicating the proximity to several of the areas where Joseph worked with the partisans, especially Naliboki Forest and Baranovichi. (Sketch by Pat Jackson.)

Kozhany Forest

✶ Vilna

KOMMISSARIAT   Naroch Forest

OSTLAND   Minsk ✶

Lida ✶

Naliboki Forest

✶ Novogrudok

✶ Diatlovo

Derechin ✶

✶ Baranovichi

Lipiczany Forest

Mogilev ✶

UNDER

GERMAN

MILITARY

ADMINISTRATION

vsk

REICHSKOMMISSARIAT   UKRAINE

✶ Rovno

CHAPTER FOUR

HOME TO MINSK

J oseph might have had a sore butt as he was leaving Poland, but he was a hero in Russia. During the war, whenever he had done something exceptional for the partisans, such as lead groups to safety or show the partisans a good place to blow up a railroad track, a message describing his achievements was always sent to the authorities in Moscow. After liberation, Joseph received medals for his accomplishments, reflecting both "partisan first class" and "partisan second class" awards. Put altogether, Joseph says modestly, "they weighed a lot."

Of course, his mind was not on medals when he got back to Minsk, still in the company of Yakubovski. He wanted to be reunited with Rachel and Leva. He reckoned they were somewhere still with Zoring's group, but it had been quite some time since he had heard from them. One day Joseph's mother and brother simply showed up in Minsk, a part of the thousands of refugees pouring back into the cities.

Now restored to at least a part of his family, Joseph could move out of the army barracks where he had stayed with Yakubovski, and look for permanent lodgings. This endeavor brought to mind a few matters of the past. And, in turn, these matters inspired him to implement something he had brought back with him from the Naleboki forest: an automatic machine gun.

JOSEPH I head straightway for Grushevski-Poselok, the suburb where Papa, Mama, Leva, grandparents, and I had been living when the war began. I remember all too well Mama's and Leva's torturous night walking from the ghetto back to their old home, only to be cruelly turned away by the new occupants – occupants who were supposed to have been our friends.

Now, with my machine gun (almost as big as myself), and in broad daylight, I run to our old apartment building in the suburb. I am definitely intent upon wreaking vengeance for the way Mama had been treated. I want to shoot them.

When the occupants see me coming and spot that big machine gun, they leave, running as fast as they can. They know exactly what is on my mind. I chase after them, firing my gun into the air and cursing them (good thing Mama didn't hear me), but they are too fast for me. I try my best to catch them.

Thank God I didn't. I am glad I didn't kill anybody over the matter of our old apartment.

A few days after the three settled into an apartment (not in Grushevski-Poselok), they had a visitor. It was Joseph's good friend and benefactor (except for the watch), Ivan Vasilievich Yakubovski. He did not want to see Joseph as much as to speak with Rachel.

Times are not easy for you, Yakubovski told Rachel, and they will not soon get better. Joseph, he explained is a teenager, and he needed to be in school now that liberation had been accomplished. Yakubovski could get him into a good school. Rachel already had one son, Leva, and Yakubovski had none. He begged Rachel to let him adopt Joseph. He promised to be good to him.

These were compelling arguments. Undoubtedly, in a material sense, Joseph would have been better off with Yakubovski than with his mother and brother. But it would have meant breaking up the Gavi family even further. So many of them had been lost in the war, and now to think of Joseph belonging to someone else was too much for Rachel. She politely refused Yakubovski, and equally politely, Yakubovski accepted her decision. "I understand," he said quietly, and left. That was the last time Joseph ever saw him.

For certain, there was one thing Comrade Yakubovski was right about: times in postwar Russia were dreadful. There were no jobs, food, or supplies to speak of, and it was as if everyone had changed their Nazi masters for Communist ones.

Rachel found a modest job as a bookkeeper, with small wages and a food allowance that was just barely enough for her, let alone Joseph and Leva. She hoarded the daily supplies of food given to her at work and brought them home each night to her two sons. Consequently, Rachel was hungry all the time, and her legs became seriously swollen. Leva was still too young to know what was going on, but Joseph knew that if this situation continued, his mother was going to die of malnutrition. Did the thought ever cross his mind that perhaps he should have become Joseph Yakubovski in the place of Joseph Gavi?

JOSEPH I thought that my experiences with the partisans might qualify me for entry into a military school. I was only thirteen years old, but already a hero of the Soviet partisans. Surely, this would get me into the school of my choice. If so, I could board, and thus relieve Mama of having to give me her food.

I knew that a school, the Suvorov Military Academy, had operated in Minsk before the war, but it had always been for big shots' kids. Anyway, I packed up all my medals and went searching for this school. Soon I found out that there was no such school anymore in Minsk. It had closed because of hostilities, with no chance of re-opening any time soon.

I was told to go to Gomel, the second largest city in Byelorussia, some 200 miles east of Minsk. I went to the railroad station, but there was no passenger car – only freight cars.

But if slipping in and out of the fences of the Minsk ghetto had been no particular problem for me, secretly getting onto a freight car headed for Gomel was a snap. With a loaf of bread that Mama gave me, and all my medals – because I thought they would be useful to me, and I was right – I headed for Gomel. My clothes and shoes were terrible. The soles were separated and I had to tie up my shoes with a rope.

In Gomel, if I had been a regular kid, no one would have talked to me, but they saw my medals and were impressed. "Why are you in Gomel?" was the first question. "To go to military school," was my answer. "But there are no military schools here," was the response. "You will have to go to Moscow."

I steeled myself against disappointment. I knew from my life's experiences that I had to keep trying. I wanted to go to a military school, and by God, I would!

Joseph stayed in Gomel for two days. The city had been liberated some five months before Minsk, so it already possessed certain facilities that Joseph found most welcome. The authorities gave him food stamps which he could take to one of several designated restaurants and have fairly good meals – at least better than he had gotten back in Minsk. There were also places to sleep overnight, again provided by the local Communist functionaries.

Someone told Joseph that he would have to go to Kiev, not Moscow, if he really wanted to get into a military school. He saved some of his food from the restaurants and again went to the train station. Once more he slipped aboard a freight car and made the trip without incident. Nobody paid any attention to him, unless he happened to be wearing his medals, when they saw him. He was just one of thousands of Soviet comrades, both young and old, getting transportation the best way they could in the postwar period.

JOSEPH "Yes!" I was told in Kiev, "we do have a military school." But not even my documents from the partisans and medals from the Soviet Union could help me. "It is already September," and the school had been in progress now for several weeks. "You must go to Moscow, where the main office for our military school is located. If they command us to accept you, even at this late date in the academic year, we will take you."

I had no choice, but I was so tired from my travels that I decided to stay a while in Kiev. I had no difficulties getting the food and housing vouchers: everyone respected me for my activities during the war.

One day, simply for a diversion from my troubles, I decided to go to the movies, to see Sadie Thompson. I showed the cashier my medals at the box office and was ushered right in. Once inside the cinema, however, I saw that all the seats were occupied. When the usher saw me standing, he conducted me to a special seat of honor, where I sat and watched the movie. At no time did anyone in the cinema demand any money from me.

During my three-day stay in Kiev I saved up food and then once again headed for the train station, this time to travel to Moscow. I found something that had eluded me so far on my odyssey: a passenger train rather than a freight car. I sneaked on board and hid in a toilet. It was not long before the conductor caught me.

"Do you have a ticket?" the conductor asked.

"No, I have only this bit of food, as you can see.'

"I knew the conductor, an old guy, could not stop the train, since it had begun to pick up speed. So I decided to tell him my whole story, as well as show him my partisan documents and medals.

"Okay, then, come with me," the conductor said.

He took me to his own cabin, a private room outfitted with a sleeping cot. I was overjoyed: the trip to Moscow, the conductor told me, would take about thirty hours, and I would be in the lap of luxury! I was in very good condition!

It was good that Joseph arrived in Moscow rested, for in this largest city that he had ever seen, he really did not know where to turn. Every person he asked had different directions to the main office of the government sponsored military school he was seeking.

The Muscovites were full of questions: "Why are you wearing such dilapidated clothes? Where are your parents? Why are you alone in a big city? Did you really fight with the partisans? Is that why you have those medals and ribbons? Joseph answered their questions gladly and fully, but one thing he withheld from his inquisitors: his Jewishness. He could not personally attest to the widespread allegations that Moscow was the most virulent anti-Semitic city in the Soviet Union, but he thought prudence his wisest course.

JOSEPH   I didn't look Jewish, and my name didn't really sound Jewish, but my intuition told me not to mention it.

Finally Joseph found a friendly policeman who, after looking over the young man's medals, ribbons, and documents, wrote down the address of the place he was seeking. "I think they will send you to the military school," the policeman told Joseph hopefully, "because you are so highly decorated."

JOSEPH But it was the same as in Kiev. "Yes son, you would be a fine military student. But the school year has already started. We cannot let you in. The school started in August and it is now late September. We can enroll you next year; that is all we can do."

At the end of my rope, I was half way between rage and tears. Sensing my state of mind, the school's secretary told me to take my case directly to the Speaker of the Russian Parliament, Michael Kalinin. "If he orders us to take you," he told me, "we will, of course, accept you." As in Kiev, I went to the central Komsomol [an organization of Communist youth] office where I was given food stamps and a lodging voucher. I quickly found a dormitory that accepted my government tickets and, since it was late in the day, I decided to get a good meal and turn in for the night.

The next morning I could not find Kalinin anywhere. The best I could do was to encounter Kalinin's secretary, a functionary named Gorkin, who assured me that he was Kalinin's second in command. In sweet bureaucratese, as I remember, Gorkin told me, "I cannot break the rules. I know you are a decorated veteran, and that even at your young age, you are a hero. But military school started in August, and you are too late now to be enrolled."

Gorkin did offer Joseph something. "We have a famous orphanage," he told the young man. "It is for children of generals and other high ranking officers and for high ranking government officials. It is nice and warm, and there you will get a good education."

JOSEPH Of course, I have not told anyone about Mama back in Minsk, for that would start background checks, which would reveal my Jewishness. But to be classified as an orphan, I believe, would be deceiving and disrespectful of my entire family. At least at this time of my life, I think so. I give Gorkin the only answer I can, "No."

Gorkin shrugged his shoulders and said, "All right. If you don't want this position, there is nothing more I can do for you." Then he turned his back on the young man from Minsk.

Joseph got as far as Gorkin's secretary's office, and then broke down in tears. He had tried in Minsk, Gomel, Kiev, and Moscow, to get into military school and had failed completely. Though he was a decorated military hero, he was still a thirteen-year-old child, and though he willed otherwise, the tears came unabatedly.

Gorkin's secretary was a kindly woman of around forty-five years, Joseph estimated. "Why are you crying?" she asked the boy. "It is a shame that a child such as yourself should have to go alone before high ranking government officials."

Joseph spilled out his heart to the kindly lady. "I have no one to turn to," he told her. He proceeded to tell her everything: of his activities during the war, and the hardships his family suffered in the postwar period, and then the bureaucratic wall of resistance and indifference to his getting into military school.

Then the unexpected happened. "Why don't you come and live with me?" the secretary asked. "I have only a daughter, no son. You come and live with me until next year, when you can get into the military school."

"Why not?" was Joseph's first impression. The secretary is in such a high office, and she can help me get into military school. I would be a fool not to take up her offer.

JOSEPH   I went to live with the secretary and her eighteen-year-old college daughter. The woman bought me new clothes, including shoes, and put my old things away in a closet.

Each morning the two women left the apartment early, the mother going to her job in the Parliament, the daughter to her classes. The only thing left to me each day was the living room sofa. Maybe it was the inactivity of it all – I have always got to be doing something. Or it could have been homesickness. Whatever it was, I knew that a life of idleness in this Moscow apartment, even for a few months, was not for me. I was a person of action, and I meant to have it.

I remembered that Aunt Liza lived in Leningrad, and I began to think of a plan. One day soon after the secretary and her daughter left the apartment, I went to the closet and found all of my old, dirty clothes that I had worn out of Minsk.

I take off my new clothes and put the old ones back on. I go down two floors until I reach street level, and head straightway for the Moscow train station. As I run along the streets, I think: I should have written them a note of thanks, and explanation for my sudden departure. But then another thought strikes me: that's dumb. I've never been to school. I don't even know how to read and write.

At the time, Leningrad was a closed city; only documented residents could go there by train or, for that matter, any other conveyance. Each train car had two doors, one on either side, but both were tightly guarded by police. There was no way that Joseph could sneak aboard.

He went to one of the doors and, sure enough, a guard confronted him. Joseph began to cry and show off his medals. "I have no family," he lamented to the guard, "and nothing to eat," and nowhere to go "except this one aunt in Leningrad." As luck had it, the guard was the internal chief of the railroad security so, as at Kiev, Joseph was taken to the guard's compartment, and he rode there for the entire trip to Leningrad.

He knew his Aunt Liza lived in Leningrad, but just where he did not know. He did know her area of residence, so he simply started knocking on doors. He asked about Aunt Liza each time he got a wrong house, and this helped him to narrow his search. One day in early October around six in the evening, he knocked on the door at a house he was almost certain was the one where his aunt lived. An "old man" of around fifty answered the door. There was Joseph in front of him, disheveled, dirty, wearing filthy clothes. The man slammed the door in Joseph's face.

JOSEPH   I knock again, persistently. Momentarily, the man appears again, bearing a large plate of bread and sausages. "Here, eat this," he says, "and be gone."

No, no, I protest. I am hungry, yes, but I don't want you to feed me. I want to find out if this is my aunt's home, my mother, Rachel's, sister.

"What, then, young man, is your name?" the man asks, still suspicious of me.

Joseph Gavi.

The man immediately let Joseph in, though Aunt Liza was still away. After the German army came near Leningrad, Aunt Liza, along with her children — as well as the vast majority of the city's citizens — evacuated into deep Russia. By the time Joseph got to her house, Aunt Liza and her two children, Fima and Natasha had not yet returned. Her husband, Uncle

Abrasha, had stayed on in Leningrad to watch after their home and possessions. He was kind and solicitous of her young kinsman who had come from Minsk to visit them.

In fact, since it was now October (1944) and getting chilly, Abrasha bought Joseph what amounted to a brand new wardrobe, including shoes. The uncle was a civil engineer and architect by trade and thus had sufficient funds. Uncle Abrasha was a soft and good-hearted person. Not only did he supply Joseph with all the necessities; every morning he also gave Joseph money for movies and public transportation.

While his uncle worked in the daytime, Joseph once again – as in Moscow – had nothing to do. He roamed the streets of Leningrad. He ate. He went to see movies. He came home at night. He went to bed. He got up in the morning. "It was all so boring," Joseph recalls.

JOSEPH One day I went to a movie and met a young man about my age, in a navy uniform. He saw my decorations and told me, "You are dumb to stay in that old house all by yourself day after day. You need to come with me, and join my ship."

Of course I was dumb. What could I accomplish by staying in that house? I was grateful to Uncle Abrasha for taking me into aunt Liza's home, but as with the secretary at Moscow I had to get away: I could not take this idle life, even for the few months that it would take for me to qualify for a military school. I needed to get an occupation; to start learning some skills that would help me make my own way in life.

I slipped out of Liza's house, and went directly to Orenienbaum, and was immediately arrested. Orenienbaum was the main port for the Soviet 'old fleet' [that is, World War II and earlier – it did not include new ship building] and civilians were absolutely forbidden to be anywhere near it. Even though I showed the authorities all of my papers, they still kept me in jail for two days, without food.

On my release, I was ordered back to Leningrad, but was dizzy from lack of food. I decided, though it was dangerous, to slip once more into the port and to try and find some food, and perhaps get a job as a helper on a ship. The duty guard, a lieutenant, stopped me at the gate and, seeing my medals and assuming I was an orphan, befriended me.

"You know what?" the lieutenant asked, after about two hours. "You are lucky. Just today about forty kids arrived here just like you. Orphaned, smart, literate. They are going to be enrolled in the Baltic Navy School, a special naval ensign school for young men. These are 'kids for the navy.' Would you like to try it out?"

At this point I would have done anything for food, even try to make people think I was an orphan, though I had refused to do just that on a previous occasion. I gladly accepted, after which I was well fed in the navy lunchroom. When you are hungry you will do many things that you wouldn't otherwise.

I learned, however, that to be accepted, you had to be literate. I was illiterate. But I lied, "Yes, yes, of course, I can read and write."

Along with the rest of the group I boarded a truck and was transported to the school, where individually we were interviewed by the 'captain of the second rank.'

I could answer the first question truthfully: "How old are you?"

"Thirteen."

The captain of the second rank spoke to Joseph about the war, and the dreadful occurrences in the Soviet Union, not the least of which had been the horrible siege of Leningrad for more than two years. He marveled at Joseph's stories, and admired him for his decorations. Then the captain of the second rank asked Joseph the question he had been dreading, "You can read and write, yes? You do know arithmetic?" And, again Joseph answered, "Yes, yes, of course I do."

But let us see, apparently thought the superintendent. On the right side of his desk were two books, and he reached over and got one of them, with the clear intention of handing it to Joseph. Just as he proffered the book to the young man, the telephone rang and the superintendent talked for over twenty minutes. When at last he finished talking, he had forgotten completely what the subject had been before the telephone rang. He said to Joseph, "Yes, okay, you pass; you're accepted into our school." This was not the first, nor the last, time that unexplainable good fortune entered into the life of young Joseph Gavi.

JOSEPH   I am happy. I have a home. I am in a military school.

91

Not as good or famous as the army one I had wanted to get into. But good enough. I have food, and a warm, comfortable place to stay, and I have good clothes to wear, and a lot of things to do. What could be better?

My luck held out. Many of my fellow students were sent to radio and mechanical classes. I went to signal school, where I was told that this semaphore means this letter; that semaphore means that letter, etc. Fortunately, I quickly developed a photographic memory, and learned all my signals in record time. In fact, it was through these signals that for the first time in my life I learned the Russian alphabet. In two months I was able to put the letters together into words; and I learned to read. And by learning to read, it did not take me long to master the art of writing.

I was the smallest of my group of students – I was still, as a thirteen-year-old, barely four feet tall. In fact, supply did not have any uniform that would fit me, so I wore clothes that were at least one and a half times my size.

I was among friendly people, but there were two things about me that I dared not tell them. One was that I had a mother and little brother back in Minsk. This school was strictly for those young men who had lost all their families during the war.

Second, in the shower room I either managed to bathe alone or keep my back turned to my comrades. I did not want them to see that I had been circumcised. Such a discovery would reveal my Jewishness, and of course, I could not allow such a thing to happen. I was afraid I would be expelled from the school or even severely punished if it were found out that I was a Jew.

On May 9, 1945 – one day exactly after the war ended in Europe – Joseph and his class of signalmen were graduated at the Leningrad shipyards. He received a special certificate for making A in every one of his subjects. He and his young comrades were scattered to the four winds, each being assigned to separate ships. Joseph went to sea, aboard a small minesweeper whose chief duty was to cruise the Gulf of Finland for mines laid by the Germans during the war.

The marines and officers aboard his ship were almost all seven-year veterans in the Soviet navy, having been drafted in 1938. It was highly interesting, even fun, for them to have a thirteen-year-old child (he turned fourteen in November 1945) among them. But such did not mean that Joseph had special privileges. He still had to serve as an adult: four hours on duty, four hours sleep, four hours, etc. The supply officer sent Joseph to the tailor at Orenienbaum, and Joseph watched with fascination as the seamster took a large uniform and methodically trimmed it down to exactly Joseph's size!

Joseph and his comrades stayed at sea five days a week. On weekends they returned to Orenienbaum. Though he was eating well and had better lodgings than at any previous time in his life, there was still an ache gnawing away at him. How was Rachel? How was Leva? He knew he could not write to them, for outgoing mail was frequently censored. And he knew it would be complete disaster if he were to get a letter from his beloved mother.

Nevertheless, he always went with his comrades, even those considerably older than he, to various Leningrad movies on a Saturday night. And after the movies, they always filled themselves with food.

And drink.

It started out at one hundred grams of vodka each day, not really very much, about three fingers to a dedicated drinker. In the beginning, Joseph refused the vodka; he didn't like its taste. "What kind of a marine are you?" he was frequently asked. "Marines have to like vodka." So he kept drinking, until he acquired the taste for it.

His quartermaster on board the minesweeper was an alcoholic. And he did not like to drink alone. Each night he sat at a table in the dining room and shouted at Joseph to join him. Even when Joseph had guard duty coming up in a half hour or so, the quartermaster always ordered Joseph to drink with him.

JOSEPH   We sat at the table, drinking vodka that was sometimes 190 proof. The quartermaster and I broke large pieces of hard bread into a bowl of vodka and then ate it with a spoon as though it were a soup. It did not take long for my one hundred grams a day to be insufficient. The amount soon doubled and sometimes even tripled. Before long I had to have one hundred grams of vodka with each meal.

Soon I become a spectacle among Leningrad restaurateurs. I appreciated the attention given to me by my superiors, and so

I begin to savor the fun that occurs each weekend, especially at Orenienbaum, when it comes to the question of who in the house can drink the most vodka.

Many times my comrades, the marines and the seamen with me, would get into extended arguments with other restaurant patrons at nearby tables.

"Listen," they would say. "This kid here knows his vodka. He can drink several glasses and not be drunk. If he does it, you can pay our whole table. Okay? If he doesn't, we'll pay for your whole table."

Of course, at least at this time in my life, I did not get drunk, because I had had at least the one hundred grams daily on board the ship for the last several months, and I was used to its alcoholic effects. It was great fun to see a young kid drink these large amounts of vodka and then walk a straight line drawn especially for the occasion. My feats were always met with great cheering and huzzahs from the restaurant's customers. To them, it was heroic. What was even more important, I guess, than being a heroic partisan with medals, was – from the Soviet's point of view – the ability to hold one's vodka.

I was happy. Ghetto savior. Partisan veteran. Highly decorated hero of the Red Army. Navy man. Someone who has been consulted about getting into the military school he really wants after his tenure at sea. Heady stuff, this, for a thirteen-year-old, in 1945.

But one day I was called into my commander's office. And what I heard, I definitely did not want to hear.

"You know what?" asked my commander, looking straight into my eyes. "You have a mother."

"I… I…" is all I can stutter. I mumble out to my C.O., "I am not…a…bad person." I do not even ask my commander about how Mama had discovered my whereabouts.

"I know you are not a bad person, Joseph. Nevertheless, here is this letter from your mother."

Mama wrote: "Dear Joseph. I am so lonely without you. I love you so much. I want to see you. We have enough food. Why don't you come back to Minsk and go to school, and then we'll be together again? I don't want to lose you. Please come back to me."

In front of his commanding officer Joseph Gavi broke into tears when confronted with this letter from Rachel, his mother. The C.O., a kindly man, told Joseph, "Think about it for a time. Take two weeks, and go home for a vacation. But come back to us, for we are going to send you to advanced school. You are going to have a great career in the navy because of your background."

"Yes," Joseph said. "I will go home." But he did not say whether or not he would return to his naval outfit. He left the question open.

His C.O. had all the papers prepared: they were similar to separation papers for everyone, regardless of country, who has ever been in the military. At thirteen it was just like retiring from military service – even for those persons who had been in the forces for long periods. "I was a retired soldier and sailor," Joseph said.

He pondered what would have happened to him if he had stayed in the Soviet navy. Perhaps he could have become an officer, but only if he continued to shield his Jewishness. Even after all these months, no one knew of his circumcision, and perhaps, he reckoned, it would be too nerve-wracking to spend an entire career trying to keep such a secret from his closet comrades.

He bade a tearful farewell to his officers and comrades. He would be back, he said, in a matter of weeks. But he and his officers somehow knew it was forever.

His first stop from Orenienbaum was the city – Leningrad – itself. When Aunt Liza met him, she harangued him: "Where have you been? You stayed here while I was away. And you left before I returned. Where have you been, and what have you been doing? We thought you had been killed, or something." It had been about two years since Joseph had originally shown up in Leningrad.

His mother, Rachel, had sent a letter to the aunt, Liza, and Liza had sent a letter to the Leningrad police, and the Leningrad police had contacted the military. Slowly, slowly, the bureaucrats learned the whereabouts of young Joseph Gavi.

He went home, back to Minsk. Altogether, he had been away for well over a year, just about two years, actually. To him, two years; to his family, a lifetime. The first thing Rachel told him was: "You have to go to school." He almost laughed.

"What kind of school?" he wanted to know.

It was now 1946 – with her oldest son scheduled to turn fifteen in

November – and Mama Rachel wanted Joseph to enter the second grade – because surely his experiences in life would qualify him to skip the first grade. Joseph agreed to enroll in the fifth grade, but then only to placate his mother.

JOSEPH   I read and wrote very well in the fifth grade and starred in arithmetic. And I thanked my naval experience for keeping me so far ahead of my classmates. I made A in every subject. I finished the fifth grade and decided, I can't be in day school, after all my experiences with the partisans and the navy. How can I get along with other fifteen-year-olds who have not had the experiences I have had?

So I left the fifth grade at fifteen. I still drank more vodka than was good for me. But above everything else, I would not continue to demean myself in a juvenile fifth grade class, when it was obvious that I knew more about life than my fellow students and most of my teachers. I left school to seek my fortune.

Ultimately, and not without considerable struggle, he found it.

CHAPTER FIVE

THE MOUNTAINS

He started work full-time and high school night-time, both making for a very long day – it was not anywhere near the situation he had hoped for. School was all right: he was in reading, writing and arithmetic classes. At least he was not with a bunch of second graders, where his mother had wanted to put him. Nor did he have to bother with "obnoxious" fifth graders who didn't even have street smarts yet, let alone know anything about being a veteran of the Soviet military.

Joseph had to work, though, during much of each day to help support Rachel and Leva, and the only job he could find was as an electrician's helper. This job entailed working eight hours a day. "It was hard labor, with a sledge hammer and sometimes with a jack hammer." He had to dig holes in the street for electrical lines to be placed. Since so much had been destroyed in Minsk during the war, it was widely considered to be one's patriotic duty to do everything possible to restore public facilities and utilities.

At six each morning he woke up, to get to his job as an electrician's helper at about seven. He usually finished this job each day by 4:00 p.m., rushed home for a bite to eat, and then started his high school classes around six. These usually lasted until late evening, and sometimes even until midnight.

Before long it was obvious that Joseph was suffering from fatigue and malnutrition. On a good day he might get four or maybe even five hours of sleep. His "lunch" during work hours was practically non-existent. He still drank vodka on numerous occasions; it relaxed him. Nevertheless, many were the times that he lamented leaving the comforts of the navy. But he felt it was his duty to his family now to remain in Minsk. He always knew that somehow he would make it in this world, but while a teenager he certainly did not have any answers.

He began to doze on the job. "I was so tired, and the work was so hard." Digging holes in concrete most of the day and then going to school for four or five hours, all with a little food and vodka, and only a few hours of sleep a night to sustain him, wore heavily on the mental and physical strength of this young national hero.

JOSEPH The foreman caught me sleeping one day, shook me roughly, and shouted: "Wake up you shirker! Wake up! I will not allow you to shirk on the job! If this happens again, I will take you before the judge!"

I rouse myself, vigorously shake my head and rub my eyes. I quickly get back on the job.

But then it happened again. And this time the foreman did take him before the judge. In the frenzy to rebuild the Soviet Union after World War II, Stalin's government decreed that workers who fell asleep on the job could be labeled as saboteurs, trying to wreck the economy. In fact, many such "shirkers" had been given hard prison terms of five years or more. Undoubtedly, Joseph thought that five years wouldn't be too bad. At least he might be able to get some rest!

JOSEPH The judge was a woman, and she stared intently at me for a while, and then turned to the foreman who had brought me to court,

"Why is this skinny little boy standing here before me?" she asked.

"Because he is engaged in sabotage against the Soviet Union," she was told. "He falls asleep on the job, thus hindering the efforts to restore our country."

She looked at me, and asked "what is the matter with you?"

"I am tired, madame. I work all day and then go to school. I don't have much food, either at home or at the job. I have to sit down during the day and get a couple of minutes of sleep."

The judge lets me go – this time. I must be careful, however, not to be brought into her court again, at least on this particular charge. It is treason to work against the government. Therefore, if she sees me again, she will give me five years of really hard labor. Did I understand?

"Yes, madame," I mutter. "I understand, perfectly."

On the way home I am crying. "Why didn't I stay in the navy?" I keep asking myself. And bitterly, "Why didn't I become Joseph Yakubovsky?"

Speaking of the navy, one day some friends and I strolled in a Minsk park. Suddenly I saw some of my old comrades from navy days. "Why are you in Minsk," I asked, astonished, but pleased to see them.

"We have a twenty-four hour vacation, and our train stopped in Minsk." And then one of them said the fatal words: "Come on Joseph, let's have some drinks."

We went to a nearby restaurant, and it did not take long for my former comrades to start their old tricks. They bet someone that I could out drink everyone in the house.

I drank and drank, and ultimately I fell unconscious. They had to rush me to a hospital where I stayed in a coma for twenty-four hours from alcoholic poisoning. This experience 'cured' me. For the next five or six years I could just smell alcohol and I would throw up.

Some time after my recovery from my bout with alcoholism, a family friend came to our house and asked me: "Joseph why do you stay in this slave labor? That's what it is, you know. Digging holes in the pavement all day long! Where is that going to get you?" Where indeed, I wondered.

"I have a wonderful job myself," the friend explained, "working for a photographic studio. And I know that they are going to engage some people very soon, in the department of negative repairing."

What is negative repairing, I wanted to know.

"No matter, Joseph, they will teach you."

But I cannot just drop my job as an electrician's helper. They won't allow it.

"That's true. You have to write and sign a petition on why you desire to leave your current job. You have to make sure that the authorities are convinced that your next job is as important to Mother Russia as the present one."

So I went to my foreman, the very one who thought I was committing sabotage because I had been falling asleep on the job.

"Write a petition," he said predictably, "and justify your position in wanting to change jobs."

This was probably the finest piece of writing Joseph Gavi had done to that time. To help produce the photographs that showed in large part how Mother Russia was recovering from the war was not the least patriotic thing someone could do. Joseph was released from his street digging job and, on the recommendation of his friend, was hired by the photographic studio.

JOSEPH   The new job was like a sanitarium. I was not tired out by working a full day; I had enough energy. I began doing better in school and besides, in this job, I made a bit of money.

Though Joseph had now found acceptable employment, things at home were still rather primitive, and neither he nor Rachel made enough money to see any prospects of change in the near future.

There was, for example, no water supply in their apartment building – a duplex that housed three other families. To get drinking water, Joseph had to take two five gallon buckets with him to the nearest community pump. He would fill both buckets to the brim with water, and then head with them for home. He was so short that he could not keep the buckets from dragging along the ground; he could not put them down. Therefore, he found the best way to carry them was to hold them straight out with each of his arms.

He had to be strong to do this, and each day after work at the photographic studio, he became a familiar figure walking along the street, taking water to his mother and brother.

JOSEPH   One day a man stopped me and said, "How many pounds do you weigh?" I didn't know. I knew I was short, not quite five feet, but I didn't know how much I weighed.

"I am a wrestling coach," the man said to me. "Anyone with arms as strong as yours, I can make into a champion."

"Well... well..." I stammered, "I don't know anything about wrestling."

"You'll have to come to me three times a week, and I will teach you."

But I have classes every day except Wednesday, Saturday and Sunday.

"That's fine. You come to me on Wednesday, Saturday, and Sunday."

And in five months – by now it was 1947 – Joseph Gavi became the featherweight wrestling champion of Minsk, and bade fare to take the entire Soviet title. He could do ten pushups with one hand.

JOSEPH   I was extremely strong, with great shoulder muscles. To me it is easy to defeat all my opponents. They were all heavier than I; yet I was underweight. They all had to lose weight to fight me. Me, I didn't have to go on any diet whatever.

Perhaps it was this heady feeling, this hubris, that got Joseph into trouble at his job. He was so enthralled to be winning wrestling matches that he took his exuberance to work with him. He soon found that his job as a photographic assistant was mundane in the extreme.

JOSEPH   Maybe I talk a lot about wrestling for the group championship of Byelorussia and yet having to work in a dull job repairing photographic negatives. My fellow workers and I sit on a bench in a darkroom and prepare some negatives and repair others. In addition to talking more than I should, breaking my co-workers' concentration, I begin to sing, mostly the old seaman's song I had learned in the navy. Many times, the foreman contacts Mama, telling her to straigten me up. "He is interrupting everyone's work," she tells Mama. "We will have to let him go if he persists in this behavior."

"But he is so happy being a wrestling champion," Mama defended me.

"That's all well and good, madame," the director shot back.

"But we have serious work here to do, and Joseph is a distraction."

One day after work I was summoned to the director's office. She greeted me: "Well, come in, sportsman," and I suspected right away that I am in some kind of trouble. "We have a ticket for you to the mountaineering camp in the Caucasus and we decided to give it to you since you are the only sportsman we have here."

I was surprised and puzzled. I didn't know who the mountain climbers were. I knew, too, that I didn't have enough money to pay expenses beyond the tickets. Plus, and this was perhaps the greatest mystery: Only a couple of days ago they had been threatening to fire me for bad behavior, and here they were now giving me a ticket to the Caucasus.

I explain to the director that I have already spent all of my vacation money – for school tuition and exams – and that surely I will have to talk over this matter with Mama.

"Yes, yes," replied the director. "Don't worry about the money. We'll keep your salary going here while you are away. It's only for a short time anyway. You are strong, a wrestler. You have great arm, shoulder, and back muscles. And you are short. You will make a perfect mountain climber."

"A what?" I asked, incredulously.

"A mountain climber, Joseph. I'm sure that is your calling."

"But I have to discuss this matter with my mother."

"Yes, you do so."

I say to Mama: "I have had this conversation with my photographic director. She wants me to go to the Caucasus and be a mountain climber."

"A mountain climber? What do you know about mountain climbing, Joseph? Besides, it would take you away from me again."

"Yes, Mama, it will, but I really do hate sitting in the darkroom with the negatives, especially when the days are so sunny. I cannot abide such a life. It is too still. Besides, I will come back soon to you and Leva. The mountains will be only for two or three months at a time, not even that, probably. Then I have to come back and work at the photographic lab."

Truthfully, I was not all that much interested in mountain

climbing. I had never given it any serious kind of consideration. But the program gave me an opportunity for a long break from the photographic studio and its director. The offer grew increasingly attractive in my mind.

"Yes, then, Joseph," Mama said. "You have left me before and come back to me. You will do it again."

After work the next day I went to my photographic director and said, "Okay. Buy me the tickets." She responded, "Excellent, Joseph! You are a good guy."

I did not actually realize just what a turn my life was about to take.

It was not just that the photographic director wanted to get Joseph out of her hair for a while. Soviet authorities were "requisitioning" recruits for their mountain climbing cadres. Each republic had a certain quota to fill each year, and for Byelorussia in 1948 the number was two. Most people did not want to serve sixty – or even twenty – days learning how to be a mountain climber. "You break your legs and arms," they protested, "or worse yet, you get killed."

But for the photographic director there was a catch. If she could not find someone to go, she, the director, would be required personally to pay for someone's train ticket to the Caucasus once a volunteer was found. It would cost thousands of rubles out of her own salary if she did not find someone to do it. That is why she was nice to Joseph in the entire matter.

Official mountain climbing in the USSR was not just for pleasure and sport – although those were major parts of it. Additionally, it was a type of training. Soviet experiences in World War II showed that its mountain army in the Caucasus had been a liability – as seen by so many injuries and deaths – because of a lack of mountaineer training. Also, early in the war, the German Edelweiss Division, made up of skilled mountain climbers, had occupied Mount Elbrus, the highest point (5,633 meters) in Europe, and had flown their hateful flag on it. The Germans apparently intended to keep the passes open for their regular armies to come through to the areas of the Black and Caspian seas.

Shortly after the war, the Soviets decided, before the general army draft, to send 16-18 year-old people, mainly young men, to perform military exercises – among other activities – in the mountains for limited times each year, starting out with twenty days, usually in the summers. This way, if another conflict occurred, the USSR would have their own mountaineers who were physically, technically, and mentally were prepared for any wartime contingency.

JOSEPH I already possess military training, so I seemed perfect for the job. I loved mountain climbing right from the start, and I did very well with it. I had no fear of the ice and snow and the big rocks.

During the first twenty days he learned his craft quickly, and was given accelerated instructions as a mountain guide. Many Soviet soldiers had died needlessly in the recent war because they did not know enough about survival techniques in the high mountains. Therefore, Joseph took numerous survival courses, as well as those that taught him how to guide dozens of people through narrow mountain passes. Showing how seriously the Soviet government took this mountain training, after the first three weeks, Joseph and his group were given another two months for practice. They hiked, helped workers at various base camps, became "deputy" guides on climbs, and in many instances were put out on their own to learn the trade.

When the full eighty days ended, Joseph went back to Minsk – but he didn't want to – where he once again took up his job as a photographic assistant, restoring scratched negatives and processing film that had been brought in for development. He could hardly contain himself through the year, even in high school.

He went back to the mountains in June 1949 and stayed until September. He had excelled so well at the job during the previous year that his superiors allowed him to be a junior member of the teaching staff itself – a position that indeed made him proud! After this mountain trek ended, Joseph was given the title, at age seventeen, Junior Instructor of Mountain Climbing. He credits his own trainers, Vitaly Abalakov, Vladimir Kzel Ivan Leonov, and other "remarkable people" for his successes.

JOSEPH For us kids these people were not only an example of mountain climbing, but what the person should strive for. Personally, with their influence, they formed me as a human being, and instilled in me the base of the man that I am today.

In the mountains that summer, I learned, you are pushed to be a good human being. You learn to help one another.

While climbing one day a student fell and broke his leg – a very bad fracture. It took sixteen hours to get him down to the base camp, and to safety. While rescuing the young student, the group's instructor took off his coat and other warm clothes and put them over the injured student so he would not suffer too much.

JOSEPH   For us young kids, this was a wonderful example.
      Since the climbers had to be well nourished to follow their trade, we ate well, better than in the past five years. I remarked to my friends that the rest of the country suffered food shortages, but not the official mountain climbers.
      Things were a bit more difficult for me than for the other climbers. I was the shortest; yet I had to carry just as many backpacks as my comrades, backpacks that had no difference in weight no matter who carried them. When a group goes to climb a mountain, if you are not strong enough or capable of doing any job that must be done, you cannot be included.

There were lowest and highest categories of climbing instructors, and by the time Joseph had been in the business for only five years, he was designated "highest." This designation came as no surprise to anyone, not even Joseph. At age twenty in 1951, he had had more life experiences than the vast majority of people in the entire world. With this promotion, he could have any post in the system of mountain climbing education he might have wanted. These positions included being a member of rescue teams, frequently called into action to bring down injured amateurs to the local hospitals, or to retrieve the inevitable fatalities that occurred each summer as tourists and pre-army inductees flocked to Soviet mountains.
      Tourist societies were formed at Baksam, Adil-Su, Schelda, Dombai, Bisenga, and other places. They were taught the proper mountain movements on grass, rocks, snow, and ice. Though these groups were ostensibly civilian, the government liked the idea of having so many well-trained mountain climbers who might later be conscripted into military service.
      The equipment these Soviet mountain climbers used was about twenty years behind the rest of the world. Ropes made of hemp, war surplus army tents that always leaked during rain and snow storms, boots that were sometimes hard to walk in because of the heavy metal spikes on their soles, and backpacks (even as late as the early 1960s) loaded down with firewood,

potatoes, and cabbage heads: these were the primitive conditions under which they worked.

His best friend in the mountain climbing society was geographer Gera Agronovski, with whom he stayed for several years. In 1953 Joseph and Gera were put into a group of six to climb a difficult mountain named Na-cra-Tau, primarily as a training exercise. On the first day the group reached the "middle island," a camp where people had gone before and left supplies for those after them. The place was so steep that you could not pitch a tent, so everyone spent the night tied to aged ropes made of hemp, which did not exactly inspire any confidence.

On July 19, the weather turned bad, with a severe drop of temperature, so they were stuck on "middle island" for three days: they could go neither up nor down. The best they could do was bide their time. They knew no one would come after them in weather this bad, so they had to stick it out.

Early on the 22nd the group, "little by little," started to climb. After seventeen hours (which ordinarily would have taken two), they reached the peak. Without delay, and especially since it seemed warmer on the south side of Nacra-Tau, they began their descent. In two hours a heavy rain set in, and by this time they had reached the timberline.

JOSEPH   We were so pleased to see the grass and we lay down in the water with the rain above us. We were so warm that we fell asleep.

The next day, the fifth day out by now, Gera, our group, and I reached a pass and were met by would-be rescuers coming up from a nearby village, and one was driving a truck. Our group climbed into the truck, and the driver handed us a huge box of chocolate candies, which we divided among ourselves. We were grateful, for we suddenly realized we had not eaten for three days. People lined the streets of the little village when we got there, applauded, and threw flowers at us as we walked in front of them. Despite these warm courtesies from the villagers, all my comrades and I wanted was to find a toilet – some of us were pretty desperate.

As Joseph explained, the principals of the mountaineering camps wrote down all the exploits of the climbers each year: how much they worked, taught, led, and what their characteristics were. After the exploit with Gera on Nacra-Tau, Joseph and his entire group were written down as "heroes."

In a way Joseph's "highest" designation turned out to be a mixed bless-
ing. He liked the attention it got him, and the admiring stares from students
and tourists alike. But, he wondered one day whether he really welcomed
all the responsibility that went with the job. In 1953 his chief said to him,
"Joseph I have a special assignment for you. One of the sons of a Politbureau
member is coming to our camp. You are to be his personal guide. And you
know what will face you if anything should happen to this guy!

As it turned out, all was well. Volodia Andreev was the son of Andrey
Andreevich Andreev, one of the revolutionaries from 1917, and now a very
important member of the Soviet government in Moscow. Joseph and Volodia slept and ate in the same tent for twenty days while going up and down
high moutains. His trade was engineering. Their mutual interest in science
and technology caused the two young men to hit it off with one another.

JOSEPH   When the season ended, Volodia invited me to visit
him in his Moscow apartment. "On your way back to Minsk," he
told me, "stop by for a few days and I'll show you around the capital city." (I did not tell him that I had been 'shown around' Moscow once before).

Though I did not have good clothes, I did stop in Moscow
after the mountain climbing season ended. I came to this large
apartment building and thought I could just find the door to his
apartment and be let in. This was not the case. As I walked into
a hallway, I was quickly surrounded by heavily armed guards and
asked, "Who do you want to see?" I was incarcerated in a small
waiting room in the building. I kept telling them I was here to see
Volodia Andreev, but the ever-present suspicious mind of the Soviets made them think I was here on less than legitimate circumstances. Volodia was out of the apartment for a few hours; when
he returned the guards checked with him, and I was released.

I had a good visit with Volodia. I remembered all too well,
however, my previous trip to Moscow, trying to get into military school, and I kept looking around on the streets, as though I
might see the secretary whose apartment I had fled, or maybe her
daughter. Volodia and I remained friends for several years, largely
because we shared a love of mountains.

You cannot compare anything with the feeling of climbing a
mountain. It makes no difference which mountain it is; you feel such

a human being. You defeat the things that are so difficult: the rocks, snow, ice, bad weather, and all of a sudden, you're on the top of the mountain! It is competition with yourself, not in the sense of being a loner, but the best competition that it is possible for one to have.

In the ghetto, in the partisans, in the navy, it was to a great extent, 'everybody for themselves.' I had become used to being a loner, to taking care of myself in any and all contingencies. But in the mountains it could not be this way. There was no such thing as 'to each his own' fourteen to fifteen thousand feet above sea level. In fact, the Russian school of mountain climbing showed 'collectivism' at its best, because single climbs were totally prohibited. This system, even with the absence of good equipment, made it possible to perform the most complex climbs with a minimum loss of life.

In the mountains people will give their lives for you if necessary. People do not climb mountains to get applause or to become heroes; that is a part of it, yes, but if it were totally so, mountain climbing would be self-defeating. You climb because of the beauty and philosophy of it all. There is the sky. There is the snow. And it's all so beautiful!

Not the least lesson from mountain climbing that I learned is that we are all related to one another; in the mountains, working relationships with each other are of utmost significance. Mountain climbing is a group activity; if you are a bad person, selfish and cheap, nobody will accept you – and word gets around very quickly in mountain climbing circles. It is good people who survive the mountains, the ones who are honest, and physically, mentally, and morally strong. If you are a complete loner, a person who only thinks of himself, you will not get far in the mountain climbing society.

Mountain climbing also taught me the value of a higher education. Each summer for three or four months I went to the mountains – and I did this altogether for nearly a quarter of a century.

It had been a struggle for me to get through elementary school – after my stint in the Soviet navy – to say nothing of high school, which I finally – at long last – completed in 1951. By then I was in my twentieth year.

I never thought anything about higher education until I started my work in the mountains. There, in the heights, I was with beautiful people, people who were ninety-nine percent university students, along with even more highly educated individuals. They incubated in me a love of learning and an almost irrepressible desire to be a teacher. Even though I had to go back to my photographic job in Minsk for the better part of each year, I began instinctively to suspect that I would spend a good part of my life in the classroom and scientific laboratory.

It was science that he loved. The thought first, then the exploration, and afterward the experimentation. It was the challenge that attracted him. He had been challenged all his life – Nazis, Byelorussian police, partisan adjustments, naval service, falling asleep on the job – in what had he not been challenged?

Joseph's tenure in the mountains each year was all too short – only three or four months during the summers. If he had his way, he would have stayed there the year round – after all, the weather did not change all that much. But he had to go back to Minsk for eight or nine months, to work in the photographic lab.

In a couple of years at the photo studio, he became a "professional," that is, he was expert at printing pictures from negatives, and repairing those that were damaged. One of the prices one had to pay for being a "professional" was to teach the trade to younger employees, to engage in a kind of "monitorial" system.

JOSEPH   One day in late 1950 my boss had said to me: "I have a student for you to teach." I tried to decline. "Boss, I don't need a student. I'm busy enough already." What I did not say was that, since you were paid by the prints you made and the negatives you saved, and not by the hour, you would lose money by working with a student. "No matter, Joseph," the boss said to me, too cheerfully, I thought. "You have no choice in the matter. It is the law. You have to take the student. You know that."

The next day a sixteen-year-old girl walked into the shop and asked for me. Her name was Ida Engels. She was nice-looking and as it turned out, willing to work hard at her photographic apprenticeship; she learned quickly. After a while, I went to her home, where I met her mother, stepfather, and brother and sister. The two of us, Ida and me, started to date in 1950, and in 1953 we married.

In 1951, after completing his high school requirements, Joseph had wanted to enroll in the Department of Energy at the Minsk Polytechnic Institute, where the entrance competition was tough. Joseph needed to pass examinations in a foreign language (he knew German), Russian, verbal and written math tests, and physics.

He passed all the examinations with fours and fives (equivalent to A's and B's in the United States). The tester, however, Professor Nichiporovich, told Joseph: "I cannot grade your work better than a three" (a C), meaning that Joseph would not be accepted into the University. Joseph pointed out to Nichiporovich that since Joseph was a veteran, the law said that all he needed for admittance was a three.

"In that case," Joseph remembers Nichiporovich [21] as saying, you get a failing grade altogether." Joseph glanced at his examination paper and saw "Jew" written on top of it.

Joseph celebrated his twentieth birthday in 1951, and if he could not go to the university, the only other viable alternative for him would be the army. He was qualified, however, as a physical trainer. He was a classical wrestler, and a mountain climber of note. He took all his documents to the Institute of Physical Education in Minsk, along with his examination results at the University. He was admitted.

For the next few years Joseph and Ida lived sparsely as he tried to attain the education that he knew would immensely better their lives. Life was difficult for the young married couple. For one thing, they had no place to call home. Ida's parents and her little brother and sister lived in one room of about 160 square feet. Joseph remembers a hallway in the structure, and off that hallway were three rooms where three different families of various sizes lived. There was no private kitchen, and it was one hundred yards to the nearest source of water, and about the same distance to toilet facilities. They could not stay with Rachel either, since her lot was no better than

---

[21] Some twenty years later, Joseph and Ida's oldest son, Isaac, showing great promise in mathematics, physics, and chemistry, expressed a desire to become a nuclear physicist. Indeed, the authorities sent him to a special school for physicists two years before he was graduated from high school.

He applied for entry into the Moscow Physics Technical Institute. On his application sheet, he had to put down his ethnic background. His application was rejected. He then attempted to get into the Byelorussian State University. Joseph asked one of his acquaintances on the committee what he thought of Isaac's chances of success in getting into the school. "He assured me that he [Isaac] would not have any problem to pass; however, when I reminded him that Isaac was a Jew he told me he needed to consult with other members of the committee." A few days later Joseph met this committee member again, who told him that Isaac did not have a "single chance" [of entry] regardless of how well he knew the subjects of the examination." Isaac then went to the Department of Hydrotechnical Construction and Road at the Byelorussian Polytechnic Institute. He was admitted. The incident only showed Joseph that "after a quarter of a century, nothing had changed in that country."

the Engels. She simply could not bring another person into her own little crowded homestead.

JOSEPH   So we got our own apartment – an apartment that had once been a sauna. It was six feet wide and twelve feet long. The 'bed' was one mattress, laid out on the floor, and there was no heat. For these 'luxuries,' I paid ten rubles a month. Because I was an A-B student at the Institute, I got a monthly stipend of thirty-five rubles. This amount, along with what Ida and I made at the photo lab got us through, but just barely.

I reflected often on the irony of my situation: in the mountains I always had more than enough creature comforts, along with food, to satisfy me. Back here in Minsk, I had little of anything. No wonder I yearned for the summertime, even wishing to live year round in a mountain setting. But I now had family responsibilities, and had to act accordingly.

Our son, Isaac, was born in December 1954. It was so cold that we had to live under blankets that we somehow were able to obtain, because blankets were scarce commodities during the 1950s in the Soviet Union. The winter of 1954 was a tough time for our little family. No heat, except that we were finally able to talk the landlord into letting us utilize a small oven, so we could at least prepare lunch each day, and get just a bit of warmth, no inside plumbing or toilet facilities, and very little to eat.

Things improved somewhat when Ida and I decided to sell the few books we had been able to accumulate. Books were valuable in the Soviet Union in the postwar period. We could read, of course, but we didn't have time. We were so busy surviving, Ida, Isaac, and me. Therefore, we took the books to a second hand store, and regretfully sold them, which gave us a bit of extra money.

Both of us felt a little bit guilty about selling books: after all, books had come to play a major role in our lives. But what good are books if you can't live? The extra money the books brought gave the three of us a few added 'luxuries' such as meat every now and then, and every once in a long while, even a movie.

When summertime, 1955, arrived, Joseph once again planned to go to the mountains, just as he had for the last six years. Only this time, he would have company: Ida and Isaac would go with him. They would stay in the base camp most of the time, but Joseph did take Ida up into the mountains on numerous occasions, a practice that lasted for the next several years. "I taught her to climb mountains," Joseph claims. And in the future, Ida's mountain climbing expertise came in handy on more than one occasion.

Joseph maintained an accident – or even for that matter, incident – free record until 1957. In that year, Joseph was "lucky enough" to be included in a group led by Leo Filimonov, who proposed to climb Mount Ushba, a "legendary" mountain in the Soviet Union. The whole event was to last for about ten days. They reached the 17,000 peak without incident, but just as soon as they began to descend, between the north and south tops of Ushba, one of their members, V. Zubkov, a painter and artist, contracted a very high fever, and developed severe breathing problems. He could move, but not with his heavy backback. Filimonov assigned Joseph and Gera Agranovski to take Zubkov down the mountain. They were to split the contents of the young man's backpack to make the load lighter for both mountaineers.

JOSEPH   We considered that the best we could do for Zubkov was to get him to some oxygen, which meant a steep decline from the top, initially almost 500 feet of sheer vertical rock. There were three now who had to get down: who would go first? Gera would go first, because he was taller and maybe stronger than I. I was also the lightest member of the group, so if I fell it would be easier for Gera to hold me, and the strain on the ropes would be considerably less than if I went first. So I held the rope for the two to descend. But who would hold the rope for me? Nobody!

It's a funny feeling, you know. You are the last down. You have to be very careful. One mistake will be your last mistake. Going last was always the most dangerous position of any mountain climbing team. But for me, this was a great honor because it meant that the leaders… could rely on my experience, my moral and physical condition, and my judgement.

We made it. We got to the village of Gool, in the region of Upper Svanetia, still 15,000 feet up in the Georgian mountains, but we were ecstatic. We brought Zubkov to a local school, where the entire village turned out to watch him get progressively better, even losing his temperature in a short while. Gera and I were at once looked upon as heroes: we were so happy that we showed off to villagers by doing ten chin-ups each in the schoolhouse, even while wearing heavy, wet clothing. 'We have conquered Ushba,' we happily proclaimed to the astonished onlookers. Finally, a truck from a lower village arrived and took Zubkov to a hospital.

Joseph's first great personal mountain trial also occurred in 1957, when his group confronted a 17,000 foot face in the Ulu-Tau-Chana. There were five in the group, with three people on one rope, with two on another. Joseph happily paired with his friend from his early mountain climbing days, Gera Agranovski.

All five reached the summit of their mountain without incident. The beginning of the descent was uneventful as well, with the three who were together getting down without any problems. Joseph felt confident, especially since he was with Gera. Gera was a tall person, and tall people could catch falling short persons better than anyone. The drop downward was steep, almost ninety degrees.

They had been warned that during the descent they would have to be extra careful because the rocks over their route were of the "easy peeling" type, and there was the real danger that the person below could be hit by falling boulders. Gera went down first while Joseph controlled the rope. Several feet down, Gera called that he had reached an outcropping. He was tall enough to touch a ledge beneath him while clinging with his hands to the outcropping. Thus positioned, Gera shouted to Joseph to start his own descent.

JOSEPH   I do. But when I reach the outcropping, I try also to touch the ledge with my feet. I am too short! I cannot reach anything! I try to reposition myself on the outcropping, but I cannot. My packpack is heavy to begin with; now it is even heavier with all the moisture it has accumulated. My fingers straighten out, trying desperately to hang on to the outcropping.

Suddenly, I start to fall, and Gera apparently does not know anything about it. I do not scream. There isn't enough time to be scared. Only when I speed by Gera in a free fall does my friend realize that I am in trouble.

Gera immediately shortens and tightens the rope, but not before I fall some ten to fifteen feet. I get lucky. Somehow, while falling I do not flip over but fall vertically with my feet down, enabling me to maintain at least a semblance of control. Gera keeps me strong within his grasp, shouting, 'Joseph, you okay?' I call back, not all that reassuringly, as I swing in the wind with several thousands of feet of space beneath me, Yes, Gera, I am all right! But let's get out of here!

Gera brought me to him on the ledge, and then carefully, very carefully, we continued our descent of the mountain. When we reached the timberline, I began to tremble, and my knees started to rattle so violently that I had to sit down to stop the shakes. Then Gera started shaking, and neither of us Russian climbers could do anything for the next thirty minutes, as we realized that one of us had just been saved from a grievous disaster.

It was almost enough to make Joseph believe that disasters come in clusters. The very next year after his and Gera's ordeal, in 1958, Joseph was included in a group of government-sponsored mountain climbing competitors, the elite of the Soviet mountain climbing corps. To participate in the mountaineering championship of the USSR, the sportsmen had to be of the highest qualifications. Joseph was honored just to be a part of it all.

In the USSR championships, they went to the ice and snow laden Djan-Tugan Plateau in the vicinity of Marshrut, where two difficult mountains confronted them: Djan-Tugan and Bashkara. Their objective was to climb 15,000 feet to Djan-Tugan's summit, and get back to base camp before all their competitors. If they did this, they would then be in a competitive position to climb Bashkara. If they got through these two mountains before all the other competitors, they would win medals, and be heroes among the hero admiring Soviet populace.

JOSEPH   Our team began to ascend Djan-Tugan at two in the morning, and by one o'clock the following afternoon, we were on the summit. Settling near the top of the peak, we ate some sweets and enjoyed a panorama of the main Caucasus range, enchanted by its beauty.

The biggest problem on the descent was that the warm weather made the snow soft and any movement on it took a lot of strength. Despite my small weight and height, I fell down into the thick snow on numerous occasions. My group got to base came, called 'The Green Hotel,' and were so exuberant about the day's activities that they wanted to conquer Bashkara then and there – the very next day. 'Nobody's tired,' they exclaimed, 'we are ready.'

It would have been against the rules if we had started climbing Bashkara the next day; we would have been disqualified from any further competition. Though the next day was one of rest, we were allowed to move our equipment closer to Bashkara, so we would not have to spend extra time and strength in approaching our course. But no one wanted to sleep; we kept sticking our heads out of our tents, staring at the stars, which we noted with interest were not blinking. This supposedly indicated only a small percentage of humidity in the air, a thought that pleased us.

The first day out, my group and I reached a ridge at the 13,000-foot marker. Since it was now six in the early evening, we decided to camp for the night. Easy enough the next day, we reckoned, to reach the summit.

We started out at two in the morning because above the way we had to go were many ice overhangs, which would start falling once the sun came up, so we had to climb before melting problems began. As the most experienced in the group, and as its leader, I stayed at the front all the time, driving heavy crampons [bars of iron or other metal bent into hooks to serve as a "grappler" or "grappling hook"] into the ice and hard-packed snow, to make it somewhat easier for those behind. We climbed all day in the increasingly steep face of Bashkara. There were no clouds; in fact, it was clear and beautiful, a mountain climber's dream. But, showing the fickle, even capricious, nature of weather, and proving that unblinking stars are not good forecasters, at around seven p.m. – we had now been going steadily for seventeen hours – it became cloudy, and began to snow. Two hours later the snow was heavy and the wind was strong. In fact, my group and I estimated the wind at seventy miles per hour, because all of a sudden, we lost our tents; they were blown away from us, and I myself was picked up in the air for a few seconds. We were facing the night without tents.

We were at approximately 14,500 feet, and the snow covered us. We had no tents, and we napped from time to time, but didn't really sleep all night long. We did manage to save a small gas stove and melted snow for tea. Without the tents providing indoor cover for us, we were vulnerable to the temperature, which we calculated to be ten to fifteen degrees below zero. We had to keep walking and thrashing around all night to stay awake and to keep from freezing. At daybreak we found some remains of our tents, gathered them up, and stuffed them into backpacks and sleeping bags, had a quick breakfast of cookies and tea, and then began moving toward the rocky tower of the summit.

It was still snowing heavily at five a.m. Nevertheless, I saw something. It appeared to me that the snow raged more below us than above. There was no way for our group to escape by going down Bashkara's face. The only salvation, as I saw it, was to push on for the summit (it was only now 500 feet from us) and then go down on the other side.

As I near the summit, I find that the rocks are completely covered with snow and ice, and I have to clear them so the crew behind can climb them. First I am doing it in gloves, but have to take them off because to climb icy rocks in wet gloves is practically impossible. We are approaching the summit, only very slowly, and, I hope, surely.

I took a calculated risk that the snow would be less over the summit, or that it would stop altogether. I was wrong on both counts.

My hands swelled, and by the time we reached the summit – it took about three hours to go 500 feet – the snow was so heavy I could not see my arm straight out in front of me. My experience of nearly a decade told me that we could not stay on the summit very long, and that if it became necessary for any rescue crews to come after us, they would have to traverse the exact route that we had taken up the face of the mountain. We stayed on the summit only ten minutes when I gave the order to start the descent. It was now about mid-day.

Our first objective was a small plateau, some 2,000 feet below, where we believed we could rest safely – forget about comfort – for the rapidly approaching night. It was so steep downstairs that each individual step had to be considered on its own merits for security before I allowed myself and my group to take it. It was painstaking and difficult work. I went first on this downward slope, hammering in pitons [metal spikes driven directly into rock through which a rope can be secured] and crampons before permitting any of the others to follow.

Finally, all in my party found the plateau, actually more a bench, a thin and narrow ledge, no more than five or six feet wide and some ten feet long, outcropping from the mountainside. I got all my group in place by eight that night. The snow still fell and all my people were scared and depressed, including me. I thought, but only to myself, that this is the end. There was no choice but to spend the night on this precarious ledge; it was now dark, and trying to descend further would have been madness.

I ordered the group to take off their leather shoes, and put them into their sleeping bags. Their feet were wet, and with temperatures hovering around zero and expected to get worse, their feet would freeze. The ledge, or bench, was so small that there was not even enough space for all five of us sit, let alone lie down. To secure the group as best I could, I hammered in some extra pitons, attached ropes to them and to my group so that if anyone fell during the night, they might have a chance of being saved.

Despite losing most of our tents, the group still had their sleeping bags. Four of us managed to recline somewhat on the ledge with sleeping bags spread across our laps. The fifth person then lay down on top of us, and in this way we had some semblance of warmth. By my directive, as precarious as it was, everyone rotated their positions throughout the night – if, for nothing else, so that no one would freeze. I knew that it was important for the group to move around from time to time during the night to retain their mobility. Otherwise, they would simply drop off to sleep and never wake up.

While in these positions, the members of the group began to reminisce about families and friends, and I encouraged this "Geoffrey Chaucer" mood. I would do anything to keep their minds off the continuing snow and the thick sheet of ice that kept developing on the bench despite the movement of human bodies against it. Also I feared that at any minute the wind would sweep our entire group off the ledge to horrible deaths below. We tried to light a fire. We couldn't. We ate snow during the night, desperately seeking some kind of nourishment. It was a perilous time, and I realized – without saying anything about it to the group – that if we did not get help from the outside tomorrow, we were doomed. I had not thought death so imminent since the time I joined Mama in the execution barn from which Greta Koffmann delivered us. There was no water or food, and the snow and the falling temperatures did not seem to be abating. All of our clothes were frozen solid.

Early the next morning I try to put my shoes on. My frozen feet are so swollen that they cannot possibly fit. It is still snowing, but even if it had not been, the heavy accumulations during the night make it impossible to have any sense of direction. What is our height? Position? What are the distances, either up to the summit or down to the 'Green Hotel?' I simply do not know. It is a terribly depressing situation.

At midmorning on the second day of doing without food or shelter, I told my comrades: Listen, our control time has passed, so try to cheer up. I meant that people in the base camp now knew that my group was overdue; they would be concerned about our safety, and probably send a rescue team. Certainly, the base camp people were aware of the weather conditions, and would surmise that my group was in difficulty. I feared, however, that the rescue team itself would be stymied by the bad weather, and decide that it was not worth risking a dozen or so lives to save five.

My words, nevertheless, seemed to be so promising that the quartet, all of whom had frozen and swollen extremities, began to scream out into the snow laden clouds: 'Help us! We are freezing! We're going to die unless you find us!' Their plaintive calls were so contagious that I myself began to shout.

It was not until around six in the morning, after at least two hours of loud entreaty, that I heard something, "JOSEPH! IS IT YOU? DON'T WORRY! WE ARE NEARBY! WE ARE COMING TO YOUR RESCUE, JOSEPH!" Those were among the sweetest words I had ever heard.

"YES, WHOEVER YOU ARE!" I screamed, "YES IT IS ME! WE NEED HELP! WE MUST HAVE YOUR HELP!"

It sounded as though the rescuers' voices were no more than forty feet away, but distances in the mountains, especially those that are unseen, can be devilishly deceiving. On this occasion, the distance turned out to be ten times forty feet. "Don't worry," returned a voice. "We are coming for you." My heart lifted.

Then the snow stopped, and for an instance the skies cleared. Far below I caught a glimpse of the wide plateau of Djan-Tugan, where many people with some forty to fifty tents – or so I surmised – were decamping, getting ready to leave the area altogether. They were going downward. Had I simply imagined hearing one of them call out to me?

They apparently had not heard us; I must be hallucinating. Maybe they decided that it was too difficult to reach us, and it was not right for even one of their group to die trying to rescue anyone else (although it was against Soviet law for one mountain group to leave a distressed mountain group). We were sure these were our last hours. We had maybe another five or six hours until we froze (our clothes had now become icy armors) to death or died of malnutrition. It was such a distressing feeling.

Everyone responded calmly to this calamitous situation. The cold was such a dominant feeling that everyone forgot about food and water. They did not remonstrate against me for bringing them into this predicament. In fact, the group became more attentive and tender toward each other as what they considered to be certain death approached.

Then, after several hours of complete silence, on into late afternoon, which, because of the weather, seemed like twilight, something happened that I have never been able to explain. I saw a head pop up over a ledge below, one that my group and I in the bad weather of the night before, had failed to see. This 'head' said, 'Joseph, can you give me the rope?' Yes, I certainly could give him the rope. I threw a rope that was all covered with ice downward to my benefactor, who secured it tightly to his own ledge.

I tied myself to the rope and scaled down – in about twenty minutes – some 400 feet, barefoot because my feet were still so swollen they would not fit into my frozen boots, to meet my benefactor, a mountain climber and good friend, Misha Khergiani.

Indeed, Joseph heard later, the large group departing from Djan-Tugan Plateau had decided, despite Soviet law, that it was better for five to die than twenty or thirty. Fortunately for Joseph and his group, Misha disagreed,[22] and with four other men, went to the rescue.[23]

The two, Misha and Joseph, talked over the situation on Mount Bash-kara, trying to determine how to get the other four of Joseph's group off the bench. His comrades may have been somewhat experienced mountain climbers, but they did not at that time have the mental astuteness to cope for themselves. Joseph had to fill in for them.

JOSEPH   I climbed back up. I tied a rope to one of my group and lowered him to the waiting Khergiani. Then I tied a rope to the next person, and so on. Halfway down the descent, Lenia Bo-ruchovich, the final one of the group to be lowered (I myself was the very last to descend) became strange, and began to gesticulate wildly. Even Misha Khergiani below knew that something was terribly wrong. When Lenia reached Misha's level, he grasped for Misha's neck, trying to squeeze it with his hands. Then he let go of Misha, dropped to the ground, and was still.

I scurried down the rope to see what was the matter. We tried to bring him back, but we couldn't. Lenia showed no signs of life. He was dead. All of us had been so close to one another during our hours of need; and we had been so near to being fully rescued! I could not overlook the irony of it all.

I learned later that Boruchovich had had previous physical and mental problems. The medical authorities later diagnosed that he had died of pneumonia, but it was clear to me that his suffering atop

---

[22] This is the way Joseph later heard the story. The group leader of the large encampment on Djan-Tugan plateau decided that it would be suicide for his team to try and rescue Joseph and his mates. Misha, however, said, "My friends are there. They will freeze if they don't get help."

Misha and four colleagues set out at two a.m. to find Joseph. They climbed a peak adjacent to Bashkara, called "The Gendarme," which blocked their view (even if they could have seen it) of the "Bashkara Tower," where Joseph and his team were stranded. When Misha got to the top of Gendarme, they found they were actually on the same level as Joseph's ledge, and not actually all that far away, at least in terms of space --some 1,000 feet. This is where they called Joseph, and Joseph answered back.

Misha and his team had to go back down Gendarme, a perilous journey that took twelve hours, and that is why he and Joseph lost voice contact with one another, and Joseph began to believe that he and his group were doomed. But, "nothing was impossible," Joseph admiringly says, when it came to Misha's ability to rescue people.

[23] According to Joseph Gavi, Misha Khergiani was "the best mountain climber in the world." He remembered the story of a few years before about Misha's being included with several Chinese mountain climbers on "Lenin Peak," when a young girl, at 22,000 feet, lost consciousness. The only thing to do for her was to bring her down, and fast, so she could regain her oxygen supply. Misha's Chinese leader told him: "Let her along. Let her die. Otherwise, she will impede the group." Misha told him to go to hell, and put the young lady on his shoulders. He ran with her for several thousand feet until she began once again to breathe. He saved her life. He was, as Joseph remembers in understatement, "a remarkable person." Misha Khergiani died in the 1960s while climbing a mountain in the Alps.

the summit and then on the narrow ledge had been too much for him. Lenia should never have been permitted to go into the mountains to begin with. His pre-expedition pneumonia weakened his entire system to such an extent that he neglected the all-important preparations of training and exercise. The project had been difficult for me and the others, especially when bad weather set in, but it was deadly for Lenia Boruchovich. He just gave up and died.

Taking turns carrying Lenia's body, we managed that evening to descend to the junction between Bashkara and Djan-Tugan, planning the next day to go on to the Djan-Tugan Plateau. There were two tents: one for the rescuers and for us survivors, and each tent could hold no more than five people. There were five rescuers, as it turned out, and so their tent was fully occupied. There were now four of us survivors, and we had three new sleeping bags to replace those we had left behind. What were we going to do with Lenia? Leave him outside, said Misha, the rescue team's leader. After all, he's not going anywhere. And neither would his body deteriorate in the cold climate.

But I cannot abide the thought. Lenia has been my friend for the past several months – not close, but nevertheless a friend. How can I leave a friend in the cold outside? Anyway, I am so tired and a little bit cuckoo for the past three or four days. I am under a lot of stress. I decide that we cannot let Lenia stay outside. It would not be right. So Lenia and I spend the night with one another in my sleeping bag. I shove in beside Lenia's body, relax, and quickly go to sleep, and sleep soundly through the night. What is so strange about this? Nothing, really. After all, I have seen many corpses before. To shy away from Lenia after being in the Minsk ghetto and serving in the partisans would have been totally out of keeping with my training and experience. Besides, it simply is not right to let Lenia stay outside in the cold.

But the climb up this mountain and Lenia's deaath had additional repercussions for Joseph Gavi. He was stricken from further Soviet mountain climbing competitions for that season, which were to take place in the Caucasus. If he had competed in the Caucasus he might have won some kind of medal in the medal conscious Soviet Union. "If not for this accident," he says [of Lenia's dying] "I would have won medals."

Joseph did not feel any particular guilt because of Lenia. "He died not because of me but because of his physical condition," he explains. "It's still a terrible feeling," though, because when you are the leader and someone dies in your group, you are affected."

Definitely, noting the condition of Joseph's and the survivors' legs and feet, one would have known immediately why they could not go on to further competition. Their toes were already black from the exposure to snow and ice, and "you could see the difference between the dead and live skin."

A physician at the camp told them that probably amputation would be necessary, a statement that quickly and definitely caught their attention. To a person, they protested the medical man's suggestion. "Well, maybe we can save half a foot on each of you," the callous doctor then remarked.

Luckily, several British mountain climbers were nearby, and one of them examined Joseph and his group. He looked gravely at their frozen extremities. Joseph was somewhat comforted by the Englishman's presence: he appeared to be highly experienced in mountaineering ways.

JOSEPH   "What did your camp doctor say?" the Englishman asked me.

He said, probably, amputation.

The only response from the British physician was a long, "Hmmmm." And then, "let's see here."

The Englishman had an ointment with him that looked just like vaseline. "Let's try this," he said reassuringly, "for twenty-four hours. If it doesn't work, then we'll have to go for amputation. Otherwise, you will all die."

He smeared heavy coatings of this, what I called petroleum jelly, all over our legs and feet. It didn't take twenty-four hours; just twelve hours later my feet were turning rosy. Some of my associates' injuries were also already in the process of healing. It was a miracle salve,[24] at least on this occasion, and I have always been grateful that the Englishman was there to help us.

All through the ordeal, during those times that Joseph believed he was

---

[24] Actually, what the Englishman rubbed on their feet had to be some kind of antibiotic ointment. If it really were petroleum jelly, its value to the frozen feet was that it gave the skin some much-needed insulation from the elements and also some moisture. Petroleum jelly, while offering comfortable benefits in these circumstances, could not have "cured" frozen extremities.

living his last moments, he constantly thought of his young wife, Ida, two thousands miles away in Minsk. She was six months pregnant with their second child. He regretted more than he could say leaving Ida forever, and not ever seeing his newborn child, Alex, who would be their second son. During the times he drifted off to sleep on that ledge and then later on the plateau, he dreamed of Ida.

And Ida dreamed of him. She saw Joseph wearing only shorts, in a desert of snow, deep and high up in the mountains. She was sixty feet away from him and saw him extend his arms to her and ask for help. She tried to come closer to him, but each time he was pushed away by wind and snow.

All day at home Ida fretted about the dream she had had about Joseph. Her pregnancy, she knew all too well, caused morning nausea, so perhaps her physical condition brought on the dream. But the next night it occurred again, exactly as before.

She awoke at dawn and raced to Rachel's house with five-year old Isaac. "Just watch after Isaac for a while, and loan me a bit of money," she breathlessly instructed Joseph's mother, "and don't ask any questions." She rushed to the Minsk airport and bought a ticket – which she could ill afford; in fact, she spent all the money she had – to Nalchek. From Nalchek, she caught a ride with a truck driver, piloting an old Studebaker, to the base mountaineering camp known as Spartak, still some one hundred miles away, a journey that took twelve hours.

When she literally stumbled into the base camp (to which Joseph and his colleagues had now been brought), the astonished director recognized her from her previous years of climbing. He asked, very loudly:

"WHO SENT YOU THE TELEGRAM?" It would have been quite illegal for anyone to have sent Ida a telegram informing her of the plight of her husband, such was the secrecy prevailing at that time in the Soviet Union, particularly when there were deaths involved. Also, the entire mountain climbing program – or, at least its quasi-military aspect in training some of the pre-draft teen-agers – was confidential. (Joseph was thoroughly checked out by the KGB before being officially accepted for the job. Anything concerned with maps in the old Soviet Union had to receive a "top-secret" clearance). His background in the Partisans and his naval services helped considerably to gain these clearances).

"No one sent me a telegram," she replied. "I just knew that my Joseph was in trouble."

"They are alive," the camp director told her. "One of them died, but the others are fine."[25]

JOSEPH   I really do believe I am seeing an apparition. I shake my head several times, and rub my eyes. It looks just like Ida standing there, this form that I am seeing! After a while, she says to me, 'Yes, Joseph, it's really me.' We embrace.

The incident has forever after caused Joseph and Ida and most members of their families to believe in Extrasensory Perception. What was it but ESP that caused Joseph so long ago to keep dreaming about the upcoming Nazi atrocities? What was it that caused Ida to dream of her beloved husband, Joseph, in danger in the Soviet mountains? Surely, they began to believe it was within the realm of possibility for one brain to communicate with another. Who is there to say not?

JOSEPH   My group and I had one remaining problem. We had left our own sleeping bags and other equipment on the ledge where we lodged the night before Misha Khergiani and his group rescued us. By Soviet law, if these could not be recovered, we would have to pay for them. So some of my friends told me they would go back and retrieve these materials. I wanted to go with them. My friends said no.

I have to go back, I said. If not, I will never be able to break myself from being scared to climb a mountain. I have to do it. So intensive were my entreaties that the group allowed me to go with them. While Ida waited at the base camp I once more ascended the heights only a week or so after my ordeal. The group and I found the paraphernalia we were looking for, and the next day we were back at the base camp with it.

After resting for a few days at the base camp, and each catching up on family news – Joseph in the mountains and Ida with what was happening in Minsk – the young couple began their two thousand mile journey back to Minsk.

Both of them thought that everything that could happen to them, had happened.

They were both wrong.

---

[25] Ida Gavi related this story to me in an interview in April 1997, in Louisville, Kentucky.

CHAPTER SIX

COPING WITH THE SYSTEMS

I da and Rachel had never actually told Joseph that they thought he should quit the mountains, but they did give a few hints here and there. Joseph and Ida had a young son, Isaac, and now a second one, Alex, and perhaps Joseph should become more of a family man? Not that he wasn't already.

But quitting the mountains would be so hard to do. The mountains were "just one clear window in the whole Soviet Union life. In the mountains, "you could view yourself as a human being." In the end, a compromise of sorts was worked out: Joseph would go to the mountains only periodically. And each time he did he could take Ida and the boys with him, except in 1973, the year his mother, Rachel, died.

Though primarily an academic from 1956 onward, Joseph Gavi still remembered his time in the mountains. He greatly cherished the rank of captain, which his climbing comrades bestowed on him.

He had finished his baccalaureate degree in 1955, and become a part time teacher in the Minsk Physical Culture Academy. By 1961 he was a full time teacher in the Byelorussian Polytechnic Institute, and a part timer at Byelorussian University. By 1977 he had completed his Ph.D degree in physiology at the Minsk Institute of Physiology of Byelorussia.

He loved teaching. He had an excellent rapport with the students.

They were young, and physically and mentally strong. So was Joseph; he was only a few years older than his students.

But, luckily for Joseph, he was not yet done with the mountains. After only two years of full time teaching, he had an opportunity to spend his summer vacation in the Soviet mountains bordering Afghanistan and China, this time on a secret KGB mission. On the surface, it was a topographic expedition, manned by released prisoners (not political prisoners, but those in jail for robbery and burglary), for they were the most willing to undertake the work, which everyone, including Joseph, reckoned to be dangerous. Since Joseph's job was to make the mountain climbing part of the expedition as safe as possible, it was only some time later that he learned why it was "secret."

Above all else, the pay for this expedition was enticing to Joseph. For this one summer's work he would receive 400 rubles a month. In other words, he could earn two years of teaching salary just by going on this one expedition.

He and his mountain climbing friend from Minsk, Yuri Volkov, offered their expert services to the authorities, and within a fortnight, both were accepted. They would be a part of a group going into the Pamirs (a mountain range in central Asia, lying mostly in modern day Tajikistan, Pakistan, Afghanistan, and China. Radiating from it are the historical heights of Tian Shan, Karakorum, Kunlun, and Hindu Kush).

Since Joseph was the chief of his group, he could engage additional personnel. He therefore hired Ida to come along as the cook, "because it was such an excellent opportunity for us to make money." Joseph and Ida left Isaac and Alex in Minsk with Rachel, and headed east.

The government sent the couple plane tickets to Tashkent, and they remained in that historical place for two days. They wanted meat, but all they could find was horseflesh.

JOSEPH I had never eaten a horse; I cannot accept horsemeat. So we ate soup and potatoes.

And fruits and vegetables. The war had been over now for eight years, but food scarcities continued.

Never in my life have I seen so many vegetables and fruits. It was beautiful for us! The watermelons were so big – thirty to forty pounds, even – that we could hardly carry them. We finally rented a sled to pull all the watermelons, canteloupes, grapes, and apples

back to our tent room, where we feasted. We don't need meat, I told Ida, with this kind of food.

The young couple was fascinated by seeing people from nearby villages congregate in the big department store at Tashkent. Women, instead of wearing earrings, wore military buttons in their ears. Many of them had braided and pig tailed hair, held in place not by ribbons and bows, but by lavatory chains. They wore such clothes as Joseph had only seen in the movies. The two were totally enchanted by such a fascinating and historical place as Tashkent.

Their next destination was equally exotic: Samarkand, the old capital for the Mongol invader, Tamberlane! They slept in tents during the week they were in Samarkand, with hungry jackals paying them nightly visits, disturbing the couple's sleep until driven away.

Joseph and Ida may have been among the very last people to see buildings that were thousands of years old, about to be torn down by Soviet authorities in the name of "progress." They saw cemeteries they guessed to be at least 2,000 years old, being ripped up for whatever treasures might have lain inside. True, Joseph considered, it was a hard life in the postwar Soviet Union, but it was still sad to see all the old relics destroyed in the name of survival itself.

After a week in Samarkand, Joseph and his party climbed into trucks, and departed for the mountains. There were six people in his group: Joseph and Ida, the chief of topography, and three released prisoners who already were beginning to wonder whether or not they should have stayed in their jail cells. They brought six horses with them, along with food supplies: canned beans of various descriptions, split peas, barley, and pork, primarily for the prisoners and topographer, and oats for the horses.

It took two days of grueling travel to get them into the part of the Pamirs they proposed to ascend. At 13,000 feet they passed the last Soviet village before the border with Afghanistan. At the village they abandoned the motorized vehicles and the party mounted their horses, because no truck could get through the ever-worsening terrain.

After some twenty-five miles, they found a little creek, and here they made base camp. They were now between 16 and 17,000 feet, with plenty of snow and ice to make their lives uncomfortable. Ida set up cooking facilities, and Joseph decided that his wife would stay in the base camp while he and the others went up on the mountains, for three to five days at a time. Their mission was to take wood and cement, on the backs of their horses, to upper levels, and implant various surveying equipment, including numerous tripods, into the mountain, presumably so that the Soviets could get an instant "property" check in any future challenge from Afghanistan or China.

Back in Samarkand, the authorities had given secret maps to Joseph. These were precise, showing exactly where his group should go on the border with Afghanistan. If Joseph were to lose these maps, he knew he would face fifteen years in prison. The Soviet authorities believed that the only way one could lose such valuable material would be by design. Losing the maps would be traitorous to Mother Russia and thus punishable by prison terms.

On the way up, Joseph marveled, and expressed disgust, at the type of equipment the other people in his group had been issued by the KGB authorities. He had brought his own, so he did not worry all that much about himself and Ida, but he had trepidations about the ropes and other apparatus used by his colleagues.

JOSEPH   **If this is such an important mission, and I could spend fifteen years in jail just for losing some lousy maps, why did they give such terrible ropes to the people with me? I could not possibly save their lives if an emergency arose.**

Nevertheless, the money was good. Four hundred rubles a month! That was worth all the danger!

The base camp where Ida stayed behind, "was like a desert, little wood, no grass, actually not much of anything." There was the creek, however, and on its banks were numerous tree stumps from which she carved wood for cooking.

One time, Joseph and his colleagues returned from a mountaintop, and Ida had a story to tell them.

"Around three this morning as the sun was rising," Ida told them, "I started to feel that somebody was near my tent."

She was, of course, alone. She had a rifle, "but she didn't know how to shoot it." She had a knife under her pillow, "and, of course, she had never used a knife to defend herself." With no usable weapons, Ida slept in her sleeping bag, wearing a sweater and pants to help stay warm.

"Hello, lady!" some guy with a beard called to her.

"Hello," Ida said, timidly.

"Where are the rest of your people?"

"They are only gone for a couple of hours; they should be back any minute," she replied unconvincingly.

"Don't worry," the man said. "We know they will be back in a couple of days. No one is going to do anything to you. We are from Afghanistan."

Her visitors were a mullah and a dozen of his followers, all from a nearby village across the Afghan border. They were a part of those groups of nomads who travel at will without molestation between and among the borders of Afghanistan, Pakistan, China, and Russia. They have done so since time immemorial.[26]

Most of the mullah's company were children. They could not speak Russian and Ida could not speak Afghani, but they got along famously. She gave them pencils and demonstrated their uses, and buttons that had fallen off Joseph's and his comrade's shirts.

The only untoward thing that happened was that some of the children tried to drink the kerosene stored in the back of Ida's tent. She dissuaded them, giving them instead lemonade and tea flavored with many cubes of sugar. Needless to say, Ida and the kids became the best of friends.

The mullah and the children were just stopping off at the base camp for a rest. After a half hour they moved on. But as time passed, and they continued to come through the base camp, each of their visits increased to three and four hours. Back home, the children began to tell their parents about the "lady who lives alone in a tent." The mullah said, "Ma'am, you are good to our children. We thank you. Nobody will bother you while you are here. If you need something, just tell us."

The promise of help and friendship came in handy just a few days later. Joseph's company needed some two by fours to complete the triangles where the tripods were to be located. A helicopter came in, loaded with two by fours and dropped them, but not very precisely. In fact, they were scattered over a wide area. Some of them fell within the limits of the mullah's village. The mullah had them all gathered up – "though lumber in this part of the world was like gold" – and brought to Joseph's base camp. "They didn't have to do it. But they were so honest. They could have sold it or used it, but they did not."

After the lumber delivery, apparently Joseph's company back in Samarkand forgot about him and his mission. The radio went out, so communication with Samarkand was out of the question. Quickly, they ran out of medicine, so Joseph reminded his climbers to be especially careful. But

---

[26] For further information about these fascinating nomads, see James A. Michener, Caravans.

then, most disturbing, they began to run out of food. And there was nothing for their horses either.

Joseph therefore decided to gather up several of the two by fours and take them to the nearby Afghan village and try to trade them for food. Joseph, Ida, the topographical chief, and the three prisoners walked into the village, looking at everyone in sight and being looked at in return.

The chief of the village invited Joseph and Ida to his home. It was bigger than everyone else's in the community, and surrounded by a twelve foot tall fence, onto which six young women held and gaped at the "foreigners." Altogether, Joseph reckoned the chief's front and back yards to cover about three acres.

The Russian-speaking chief was in his mid fifties, Joseph guessed, accompanied by his wife of around fourteen. A second woman, presumably another wife, of about twenty-five, served them sour milk and other delicacies. Ida was permitted to sit with Joseph and the group of gathering men on the floor, on thick pillows, while the chief explained life in Afghanistan, particularly as it related to the ancient nomadism in that country and other parts of Asia, where passports were neither expected nor wanted. All of the countries in this part of Asia gave absolutely free passage to every member of the nomad tribes.

Finally, the chief took on a serious tone, and said to Joseph:

"You know, you are hunting a lot. I know you need meat."

"Yes," Joseph replied. "We are running short of supplies. We will be in desperate shape soon if we do not hear from our headquarters in Samarkand. I am sure they have not forgotten us." And then in a forlorn way, he added, "at least I hope not."

"I am certain," the chief went on, "that you and your group need pork."

The answer was an enthusiastic "YES!"

"I cannot give you the pork," the Moslem leader told him, "because I cannot personally eat it. But I can show you the places in the fields where the hogs come. They invade our fields of corn and beans and destroy them. You can go over there and kill a couple of them. Every year at harvest time our villagers go to the fields and guard against the wild boars. You do know that they are very dangerous, with long, sharp tusks? They weigh from 250 to 300 pounds, but with quick and accurate rifle shots, you and your group will be all right."

"All right?" Joseph was not at all convinced.

But after supper, the chief led them some twenty minutes out into the fields, and there they found trenches. "You can sit in the trench," the chief said, "and at one or two a.m. about thirty or forty wild hogs will pass through here." It was a long wait, considering that it was now only early evening, about six p.m.

JOSEPH We got into the trench and waited and waited and waited. Suddenly, there was a stirring. I thought the pigs had arrived early. I straightened up and saw seven local adults and several children surrounding us. The visitors threw a thick carpet down onto the ground and sat on it. They had sour milk in clay pots, and pita bread with them, which they spread out in the middle of the carpet. They invited us to join them in peace and fellowship.

We did, but before partaking of the food, the Moslem men began to pray, so my group, Ida, and I stood by respectfully until they were finished. The Moslems gave the first offerings to me and Ida. They did not know that we were Jews, but somehow the full-moon night was so beautiful and meaningful that I considered that even if they had known, it would not have mattered. At least the thought was beautiful.

We sat in the bright moonlight and told stories to one another. I talked about the recent war, always careful to conceal my Jewishness, and about my time in the Soviet navy. The Moslems talked of their heroes. I noted the profound respect that the youngsters had for their elders, and was impressed. It was one time in my life experiences that made me very respectful of the Moslems. All of a sudden the Afghani Moslem leader (probably a shepherd) said it was time to go, and at ten p.m., they departed, leaving us literally reeling from a night of pleasure.

We went back to our trench, waiting for the hogs. It was unbelievably quiet. At an elevation of 15,000 feet, the stars were as big as quarters. There was no pollution whatsoever, no dust; it was completely clear.

At about 12:30 a.m. we heard a rustling. "Something is coming," one of the company quietly exclaimed. By now, the moon had disappeared and it was quite dark, and we could not see clearly at all. It sounded like a hundred horses coming at us.

An old person from the village had told us that if you shoot at a wild hog, make sure you kill it. Otherwise, it will come after you, and you are dead. When my group sensed that the hogs were close enough, we began to fire. Each of the six made a shot, and then we all collapsed on the bottom of the trench. We believed that the hogs would shortly be coming after us. But the noise abated, and finally disappeared altogether. Ida and I and the others lay in the trench for the rest of the night, anxiously awaiting dawn, to see if, and how many of the boars, we had killed.

When light spread over the horizon, we carefully looked out of our trench, and after much investigation, we discovered that we had killed:

NONE!

When they went back to the village, an old man told them that to hunt wild boars at night is most assuredly the wrong way to do it, simply because it was so easy to lose track of the creatures in the dark, and be seriously injured or even killed. Accordingly, Joseph's group no longer tried to kill wild hogs. Instead, they became interested in groundhogs.

Another old man in the village told them: "I have severe back problems, and I have found that wrapping myself in groundhog skin eases me considerably." If Joseph and his crew would shoot groundhogs, they could eat the meat, and for the skins, the old man would bring ample supplies of potatoes. This sounded ideal, for it was vegetables, especially potatoes, that Joseph and his group wanted. (It was only much later that it crossed Joseph's mind that these old men of the village, including the chief, were probably just pulling his leg).

JOSEPH We shot a couple of groundhogs during the night, and also a porcupine or two. Everyone ate the meat, but I was put off by it as much as by the horseflesh back in Tashkent. I couldn't do it. I did save some spines from a porcupine we caught and later brought them with me to America. Isaac made a clay porcupine and put the spikes on it. [Isaac still has the clay porcupine with Afghan needles today, in Louisville]. I did relish the potatoes, however, and the fresh bread Ida made from the flour the old man gave us.

Soon back in the Pamirs, one day we were stopped by the Afghan border guards. I explained that this was a topographical expedition and, showing our papers, the guards were convinced of our authenticity.

Then I ask a question about something that has bothered me all along: What is the big deal here? Why is everything, including my mission, secret? I don't see any guns or troops anywhere. In fact, I don't see anything but a lot of mountainous wilderness.

A guard takes me aside. "That is the secret," he tells me.

"What?" I ask, astonished.

"That there are no soldiers or guns or bullets whizzing all over the place. We just want other countries to think so."

I nearly laugh. So this is the big secret!

By late August their job in the Pamirs was almost completed, and Joseph knew that in early September he would have to be back in the classroom. Legally, however, he could have received released time from his Institute until he completed the job in the mountains. He could not have been punished by academic authorities if he had stayed away. Nevertheless, he and the topographer considered that one more ascent to the top of the mountain was necessary.

On this last trip to the top, Ida went with them. Just before a very steep grade, Joseph tried to get the horses to go straight up, in the interest of time and efficiency. The horses balked. They would not move. Finally, Joseph Gavi figured out that the horses were used to serpentine routes up mountains. When he gave them their head, they accommodated him. Five of the horses carried cement, lumber, and other equipment to be used in building triangles at apexes in which to implant the tripods and equipment used for measuring elevations.

The sixth horse was for Ida. Joseph walked in front, leading the horse, "because there was no road, just wilderness." On the second day, going up a sixty-degree incline, Ida called out to him:

"Joseph, I am sliding from the horse. Joseph was tired and ill-tempered – maybe it was because of the porcupine or the boars – so he yelled back, "shut up and sit on the horse. You'll be all right."

Then suddenly there was a great shout from the other men in the group. They discovered that the saddle girth on Ida's horse was broken, and she really was sliding from the middle of the horse to its rump, and coming perilously close to plunging two thousand feet back down the mountain. "Another two or three minutes," Joseph recalls, "and she would have been killed." The group stopped and repaired her saddle. Ida was in tears, reproaching Joseph for not paying enough attention to her. He did from then on – and has ever since.

At the top of this mountain, Joseph and Ida, three prisoners, and one topographical engineer, were absolutely certain that they were the first people in the world ever to be there. Were they in Russia or Afghanistan? They neither knew nor cared. There was no grass in the area, only rocks.

Joseph had now mounted a horse, better and more quickly to survey the top of the mountain and surrounding areas.

JOSEPH   My horse could not find enough ground for a firm grip, so it slipped and began sliding down the mountain on its back with me, at the beginning, on top. Then the horse turned, and I slid along on the stones under it, like a meatgrinder, until there was no skin left on my entire left side. Finally the descent stopped, and I, injured and in pain, rose to my feet and dusted myself off. I was bleeding, and it stuck to my clothes and caked my skin. There were no medicines to relieve my pain.

My colleagues urged me to return to base camp, but I knew there was at least one more day's work here in the mountains. Besides, I knew that if I descended now, I would never again get a mountain climbing job.

It was one of the most miserable nights I have ever spent. I could not remember any night, even during the war, that was worse. We camped out at the base of the peak, in tents. We had no skillets. Ida mixed some flour and water – that is all we had – and found a flat stone upon which to put the mixture over a hastily built fire, and hoped for the best. Her pancakes that night were so bad that not even the horses would eat them.

During the night I could not sleep. We were almost at 18,000 feet, and my wounds from the falling horse gave me chills and a fever. Sometime in the early morning, well before dawn, I arose and looked out of my tent, and suddenly my insomnia and pain no longered bothered me.

My God, I exclaimed. I have climbed the mountains many times, and I have watched the wonderful stars. But NEVER LIKE THIS! You can almost touch them! They are so big and clear. The air was dry – no moisture at all. Everything is so precise and sharp!

I was so excited that I woke up everybody in my camp.

Just look at the stars, I shouted.

'Shut up,' said a colleague. 'We see this stuff everyday.'

I woke up Ida to show her the beautiful stars, and she was glad to see them, and to know that I was not suffering from my wounds all that much.

At dawn I awoke again and prepared some tea: mostly hot water with cubes of sugar in it. Everyone felt so well and upbeat that they actually ate the rest of the pancakes they had scorned the night before.

Our mission on this last day of our assignment – at 18,500 feet – was to make a flat space with a hammer and chisel on which to put the triangle and then the tripod. We did everything we were supposed to do, measured the elevation, and then we were done.

As we began our descent, my euphoria about the previous evenings' stars began to fade. My pains returned, and I felt a sincere sadness of loss. This was it; this was the end of my summer expedition, and perhaps my entire mountain climbing career. I would now have to return to the mundane duties of the classroom. I loved teaching; nevertheless, I hated more than I could say leaving the mountains once again. In my mind, I was already making plans for my next mountainous adventure.

It took a day and a half to travel back to their base camp. After resting for a day, the group then made their way back to the Afghan village, taking some more groundhog skins to the old man. Joseph hoped this would induce him to furnish them with trucks or an automobile with which to go downstairs to arrange for transportation back to Samarkand.

A woman of about thirty appeared while Joseph was giving the groundhog skins to the happy old man. In her apron she "was collecting the droppings of the horses and cows nearby, to be used for building cooking fires." She deposited the cow patties on the ground near the fire, and told Joseph "I will bring you and your group some food." She reappeared a few minutes later holding all sorts of vegetables and fruit in the very apron she had used a moment ago for cow and horse dung. Joseph and his group were so hungry that they ate the food anyway.

In the corner of the old man's tent were huge stacks of pillows and blankets. Joseph and Ida were invited to spend the night. Gratefully, they did. Then, over the next several days, by auto and air, they made their way home to Minsk.

He did, of course, enjoy the extra money from his "secret" mission ("I had never seen so much money in my entire life"), 1,200 rubles, he and Ida earned that summer in the mountains – and felt so "rich" that he planned to buy a small refrigerator with it – but still, a family of four found it hard going on 125 rubles a month. He did buy a refrigerator, but to speed up his place in the waiting line, he had to pay double its normal cost.

Joseph's uneasiness about getting back into the classroom turned out to be well founded. All of his colleagues knew he was a Jew, and he had excellent relations with his students. But as always it seems, a few in his department ridiculed him, and tried to keep him from progressing. There was no tenure at his university; he had to sign contracts – based upon the recommendations of his colleagues – for five years at a time.

JOSEPH   No matter how hard I try to befriend them, two of my colleagues always belittled me. No matter how hard you try, how much time you spend in class, how much you contribute to the department with good teaching and research, it doesn't matter. I am a Jew, and to these two, nothing else mattered.

At first I simply shrugged it off. I was young and physically and mentally strong. I had fought for my country and I definitely believed I had a place in the new Soviet society. Am I a Comrade because of my special status as a veteran? And because of that, will my Jewishness cease to be a concern of anyone's? Was I first a Comrade or first a Jew? Why couldn't I be both?

But as time passed, I discovered that I was naive. The situation disillusions me. Although I had done right by my country during the war, I slowly and painfully discovered that loyalty in the USSR was not a two-way street. I actually began to have thoughts of whether or not I would again even offer my life for my country.

One day in a departmental meeting, one of my tormenters told an anti-Semitic joke, all, I suppose, for my benefit. I stood up and confronted him. I understand what you are doing, I told him. You are anti-Semitic. You don't like me because I am a Jew. But I am not going to take any more of this behavior from you. I contributed to my country during the war, and I am decorated by my

Joseph Gavi, 1955; 23 years old.

Above: Ida with the children in a mountain climbing camp.

Right: Ida with Isaac and Alex—1964 at Red Square, Moscow. (Upper left)

Above: Isaac and Alex in Caucasus.

Left: Isaac and Alex, Jospeh and Ida's sons.

Joseph giving equipment lessons to neophytes in mountain climbing techniques.

Standing in front of Peak Shurowski in the Caucasus.

Joseph Gavi in the mountains, 1970s.

Right: A mountain road in the Pamirs, 17,000–18,000 feet.

Below: Ida and Joseph on the topological expedition. North side of the Himalayas.

Joseph in Ghiang Shan, border of China.

Joseph atop Mount Elbrus, highest point in Europe

Joseph being greeted by mountain climbing camp in 1953.

Certificate of active participation in the Zhukov Brigade of the partisans during WWII.

Diploma from the School of Military and Naval Fleet; Soviet Navy.

Diploma from the Soviet Navy–Baltic Fleet–showing completion of signal school.

Certificate of Graduation, 1951, from the State Institute of Physical Culture in Minsk.

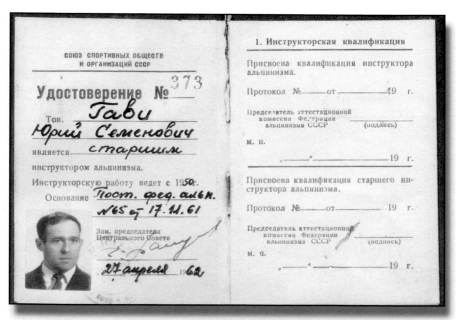

Certificate from the Union of Sports showing that Joseph is a Senior Instructor in Mountain Climbing.

Medal for partisan activities during the war with the Zhukov Division.

Camp inside Caucasus. After finishing his teaching Joseph was allowed to bring Ida and their two children to camp with him for a while. Gavi Collection.

Minsk. Sovetskaya Street near Komarovskaya Square (now F. Skorini Street near Y. Kolasa Square). Early 1950s.

Topographical expedition to the Pamirs.

A Russian climbing group, ascending a mountain in honor of Lenin.

Ida and the horse on the Topographic Expedition to Afghanistan.

Left to right: Arutunaian Rubek, Joseph, Ida, Alex, and a friend of Alex. Taken on the day the Gavi family departed Minsk for a new life in the United States.

Joseph (left) and his assistant in Joseph's laboratory.

Gavi's Restaurant, Louisville, Kentucky.

Sam Bird, cook at Gavi's Restaurant.

Joseph Gavi in 1998 standing in front of Chaim Livchitz 1994 painting, "Prayer in Minsk." Lincoln Terrace Art Studio & Gallery; Skokie, Illinois.

House constructed by Joseph and his son Isaac's construction company.

government, which is more than you can say. I am a loyal comrade of the Soviet Union. I do not deserve to be treated this way, and if you don't stop bothering me, I will take legal steps. The seventy odd other members of the department strongly supported me and my outburst. Many of them talked to the two offenders, and the troubles stopped – at least temporarily.

Around 1967 Joseph began to feel that teaching alone was not completely satisfying him any more. He had always wanted to do research that had something to do with mountains. He teamed up with a friend, Mecheslav Kulvanovsky, to study how the human body reacts to high elevations and low supplies of oxygen.

He made an appointment to see the director of the Institute of Physiology at the Academy of Science of Byelorussia, Professor Bulegin. "Young man," he spoke to Joseph, "what do you want?"

Boldly, Joseph told him, "I want to be a researcher in physiology. I don't need you to pay me any money. I will work in my free time if you will agree to be my research leader."

After looking over Joseph's credentials, Bulegin said, "All right, young man, come back tomorrow. Because you are friend of Professor Kulvanovsky and you can use his laboratory, I will be your leader and he will be your sponsor."

Joseph began research in gerontology and physiology, with a specialty in periphery reflexes in ontogenesis (a field of science that deals with the total biological history of an organism). He needed animals and various tools to carry out his duties, and these – but not any salary – were budgeted by the Institute. Even while acquiring a reputation as a researcher, he still taught over thirty hours a week at the Byelorussian Polytechnic Institute.

Within a year Joseph and Kulvanovsky had written an article, and he had learned how to do surgery on mice while researching peristaltic organs and electrical physiology. Even though he found teaching and research exciting and invigorating, he continued to go back to the mountains every summer, where he worked in the camps as a climbing and rescue instructor.

Within three years, Joseph had many articles behind him, some that were presented to various conferences across the Soviet Union, in cities like Gomel, Kiev, Moscow, and Leningrad. (He often wondered on these occasions what the people he met in these cities on a previous occasion when he tried to get into military school would think of him now).

Even some of his articles were orally presented in other countries – but not by Joseph! He had to give them to a colleague, who then traveled and read the paper for Joseph. Why? Because Joseph was a Jew and not allowed out of the country!

The same travel ban applied to "ninety-nine percent" of Joseph's Jewish colleagues. But they were all so busy with basic scientific research that they did not dwell on the fact that they were second class citizens. They were scholars and had no time for ethnic and political quarrels. Even so, the thought increasingly occurred to Joseph: "I am not at home."

One day Kulvanovsky asked Joseph personally to guide a few biology students through to their basic diplomas. Joseph agreed. Now he not only taught and researched – primarily in the field of physiology – he also became the personal advisor of numerous students.

JOSEPH   I was fortunate. How happy I'd be if I didn't have to make money. Just do the academic work. But, then, you know, you have to eat and pay the bills and raise the kids.

Joseph wanted his own laboratory. He was happy using Kulvanovsky's, but for the many different kinds of research he wanted to do, he needed his own place. He approached his department head, and to his pleasant surprise, his request was granted!

There was a very big field for physiological research. He wanted to embark on a new project: to see if educational pursuits affected the physical conditions of students and, if so, how. He wanted to involve both faculty and students, but his supervisor limited the experiments to the biology faculty. Most of the biologists were recent students, and they could fill out the forms to give Joseph the information he wanted.

In a year, Joseph had become the Deputy Chief of the Department of Science. This meant that every teacher in the department who wanted to do any kind of research would have to get Joseph's approval and clearance.

JOSEPH   I was hungry but I was happy doing research. The thought still ate away at me that I am a second-class citizen, but I tried not to think about it. I know that no matter how good I am, how well I teach and research, that since I am a Jew, I will never advance to the really big jobs in Soviet education.

He helped the chief and other senior professors to write out teaching plans, and continued with a heavy schedule of research. Altogether, in his teaching career, besides his dissertation, he wrote by himself or collaborated with Kulvanovsky or Bulegin on twenty-nine different scientific articles.

Some of his titles were: "The motor function of the large intestine of the white rat in 'agonizing' conditions," "Senile character changes of the motor function of the large intestine of rats," "A question of decentralized inside organs and vegetative ganglion," "The level of closing peripheric motor reflex of the intestine in ontogenesis," and "Age changes of reflex function of the mesentery ganglion." Also included were: "Age changes of the motor function in the large intestine as an index to the aging organism," and "Influence of 'gemcholing' reserpine on the reflexes of rats at different ages on the mesentery ganglion." All this, and more from a man who loved the mountains! Could his seeming preoccupation with suffering and death in his scientific research subconsciously have had anything to do with his experiences in the holocaust, and his actions with the partisans?

Joseph and his colleagues did their work on these articles in the Laboratory of General Physiology of the Institute of Physiology of the Academy of Sciences, the Byelorussian Soviet Socialist Republic in Minsk. The journal that published most of Joseph's work was Physiology and Biochemistry of Ontogenesis, headquartered in Moscow, and published by the USSR Academy of Sciences.

It was one of the most prestigious scientific journals in all the Soviet Union. Soviet scientists who wrote for this journal were routinely recognized by the world community as superior in the hard sciences. Government officials tended to like these scientists because they were obviously nonpolitical. "The best and the brightest of Soviet intelligentsia moved into such highly arcane areas because they knew the authorities, unable to understand their work, would leave them alone."[27] Even so, being a popular teacher and beginning to do notable research, Joseph still could barely eke out a living.

He urged his department head to increase his salary, to no avail. He constantly asked for a promotion, especially when he won the coveted Best Teaching award one year. Even a slightly higher position would yield 130-140 rubles a month; not much, but better than at present.

---

[27] Interview, Professor Hugh Phillips, Western Kentucky University; Cherry Hall; 15 December 1996.

His chief, a kindly, but somewhat wishy-washy, man, could do nothing directly for Joseph. But then it happened that the deputy President of the Byelorussian Technical Institute became ill with collapsed lungs, and was looking for someone who knew something about physical rehabilitation. He telephoned Joseph's department head, and the latter recommended Joseph.

"Joseph," the chief said, "we have to help this comrade. We depend on him to support our own department. Besides, everything I know, you know. You can help us all out by tending to the deputy President."

For two or three times a week, two or three hours a day, Joseph began to rehabilitate the stricken administrator, and he kept it up for two years. During the time Joseph and the school official became personal friends.

JOSEPH One day I learned that a senior colleague had reached retirement age and had announced his intention to leave the Institute. I agonized for a week or so over whether or not to ask for this vacancy. But I have been with Institute for a long time, and not received any pay raises. Life is still tough for us.

I did go to the chief. "There is an opening, and maybe you can help me. I want you to recommend me for this position that is becoming available."

"Yes," responded the chief. "Yes, Joseph, you do deserve the position. But don't forget, you are a Jew."

"But what do you think of me personally?" I persisted.

"I would not hesitate to help you, Joseph, but I will be told that we already have enough jobs in the higher positions."

I went to the Institute's personnel office. "No way," he told me, "don't even try for the position."

I went home in a bad mood, saddened and depressed that I could not get a promotion simply because I am a Jew.

"What's wrong?" Ida asked.

"I don't have a future here," I answered. "Not in the Institute, and maybe not even in this country."

After I had explained how the chief and the personnel officer had turned me down, Ida asked me:

"Why don't you go to the deputy President?"

I had thought of that, I said. But I have never asked people in high authority to help me – ever. I have done things on my own, and through my own merits.

But the children are growing, and money is getting more and more scarce. At the next therapy session with the deputy President, I – timidly at first but growing ever more bold – said to him. "May I ask you something, sir? I just don't see another way out of this matter."

"Why, of course," replied the official. "Joseph, you can ask me anything you wish."

I explained everything to him. "There is this position opening soon on the senior faculty. I am qualified, but I am a Jew, and have been told that there is no way I can obtain it."

"I had not heard of this, Joseph," the deputy replied.

"If you cannot help me in this matter, sir, I assured him, just forget it and accept my apologies and hopefully there will be no hard feelings. On the other hand, though, I simply don't see any future for me at Minsk Polytechnic."

"Joseph," the academic told him smilingly. "It's nothing. I want to help you. I am going to help you. Stop worrying."

"Okay, sir." I was astounded and not-quite-yet believing. "Yes sir, thank you very much." I left the session happy, but shaking my head in disbelief.

Two days later, the department head came to my office and said, "Mr. Gavi, I can congratulate you. I don't really know how it happened, but I have visited the authorities at least two times on your behalf, and now very fortunately, they have decided to appoint you to the vacant position. It will mean anywhere from a twenty-five to thirty percent increase in your salary."

I thanked my chief profusely. "Without you, I kept telling him, I don't know what we would have done," all along knowing that it was pressure from the deputy President that got me the promotion.

Certainly by 1967, Joseph knew how to play the Soviet academic game (perilously close to the American model as well). You appeal to your immediate superior for something and get turned down. Then, as surreptitiously as possible, you approach his superior and get the job done. But you always, always give credit for happy developments to the person next up the ladder from you. You never make an immediate supervisor lose face. To do so will ultimately get you in all kinds of trouble. So Joseph could blandly tell his chief: "Thanks for the promotion; I dont' know what I would have done without you." And he kept a straight face while saying it. Joseph remained in this position for the next several years.

In 1976 Joseph confronted his third contractual test since 1961. He had now organized a physiology laboratory and was publishing articles with much more regularity than his colleagues. However, some three months before his contractual offer was to be considered by the members of his department, he was required to attend special classes that tested his knowledge in physiology and physical therapy. This was not unusual: everyone in the department who came up for contract renewal went through this two-week ordeal. Joseph "showed his stuff" during the fortnight, and of the five subjects he studied, he came out with five As.

The director of the special two-week school strongly recommended Joseph's contract renewal in the Polytechnic Institute, plus a position with a considerable raise in salary. Joseph was ecstatic: renewal of a teaching term and a considerable raise in pay. "I was happy," he says in understatement.

But, something was afoot that he did not know anything about. It stemmed from an incident that happened well before Joseph's birth. If he had known about it on this bright day in 1976 when his contract was up for renewal with a good raise in pay, his euphoria would have been considerably dampened. This early event led to another in his own time that of itself would ultimately have far reaching implications.

Ida's maternal grandfather, Alter Greendwig (later, in the U.S., Greenwald), a handsome man, liked on occasion to go to the local tavern in the village of Shatsk, not far from Minsk. One night he drank far too much vodka and, to the accompaniment of laughter and raucous encouragement from the tavern's other patrons, jumped over the bar and drew a large, exaggerated, caricatured moustache on a portrait of Tsar Nicholas II, and in other ways showed his disdain for the "autocrat of all the Russians."

Ironically and happily, as it turned out for Alter, one of the tavern's patrons that night was a friend – a policeman. The policeman told him that after his behavior here this night, Alter had better get out of Shatsk and, in fact, out of Russia altogether.

"Where will I go?" a suddenly sober Alter asked.

"To America, of course," the policeman replied.

And so, in late 1907, just one step ahead of the law, Alter Greendwig departed Russia for America. He left behind three children and a pregnant wife who, a few months after his departure, gave birth to Sima, Ida's mother. This was now early 1908.

Alter went to New York, where he found work as a tailor. His wife back in Shatsk died, and Alter remarried. Shortly after the Revolution, in 1920, Alter's older children, Morris and Lisa, came to New York. For a while Morris worked with his father as a tailor, but then he gained employment in a restaurant, and soon afterward married a waitress named Silvia. In time Morris and Silvia moved to Florida and did well in the restaurant and hotel business. They made enough money for Morris to help his younger sister and brother, Sima and Evsey, back in Russia, with packages and money.

Morris kept up a steady correspondence with Sima after the war, and in 1967 offered her a ticket and a visa for a visit. The Soviet authorities, working in compliance with the Helsinki Accords on Human Rights, agreed to let Sima go for a visit. After all, she had not seen one of her brothers and one of her sisters now for nearly forty years.

Morris arranged for Sima to stay in commodious quarters, with a maid to help her, and she stayed for six months. Her visa expired, and she was required to leave the country.

Upon her return to Minsk, she regaled her family with "fairy tale" stories about America. "Everybody has got to immigrate," she kept exclaiming. "America is glorious! The life here in Minsk is for animals, not for human beings."

Joseph listened attentively to Sima, but at that time expressed no interest in immigrating. He was relatively well off in school, and he humored Sima by telling her that he had not yet finished his dissertation.

Moreover, Isaac was just beginning his higher education, wanting to become a nuclear physicist. He had to enroll, in 1972, in the Polytechnic Institute. He could not get into Minsk University for the same reason his father had been denied years before: he was a Jew.

Next to visit was Ida's older sister, Fania, and she stayed for eight months. On her return, she confirmed Sima's assessment to Joseph and Ida: "Minsk is not a life for human beings. It's like living in a jail." She exclaimed that, "everyone of us must leave this Russian poverty. It is time to go to a place where we do not have to be afraid to admit to being a Jew."

After a time, in 1972, Fania received a permanent visa and she and her twelve-year-old daughter, Jenia, went to Miami for good. Then Ida's sister Alla and her husband, Valery, and their son, Seava, left for America, and settled in Chicago. Thus it appeared that a goodly part of Ida's family was bent on getting out of Russia and going to the United States. Most of these immigrating Russians had exit visas for Israel; en route, however, they changed the destination to the United States. This became a very common practice among all Soviet emigrants.

During the late 1970s, the Soviet Union began to ease up on exit visas for Jews who wished to join their relatives, especially in Israel. "Family Reunification Acts" became important as the Soviet Union tried to change its image in reference to human rights matters.

It was in the framework of all this immigration by Ida's family that the matter of Joseph's contract renewal came up. In this year, 1976, most of Ida's family decided to immigrate to the United States. Her mother, brother, sister, and brother-in-law decided to take advantage of the relaxed Soviet law as it applied to exit visas, and leave the country. Joseph wished them well, without quite realizing what their exodus was going to do to his career. "Legally," he said naively, "the Soviet authorities cannot do anything to me and my own little family, because we have not made any efforts to leave."

Another matter that greatly influenced Joseph when he himself, a few years later decided to immigrate, was that Sima left behind some 3,000 rubles, calling it "Joseph and Ida money." To leave the Soviet Union always cost the immigrant dearly in registration fees, customs declarations, and bribes; and Sima, practically sensing that her daughter and son-in-law and two grandsons would ultimately come to her, gave them this "immigration fund."

Joseph was pleased with this surprise, but he worried that if the authorities caught him with such an amount, they definitely would begin to focus their attention on him. The best way to get along in Minsk and the rest of the Soviet Union, he knew, was to remain as inconspicuous as he possibly could.

Joseph thought a prudent way to handle the money was to buy a car with it. He used some of Sima's "immigration funds," as well as the money Isaac and his friend Fedia made helping to build roads to various collective farms.

JOSEPH   I considered a car an insurance policy. I might lose cash, or get into trouble with the authorities for having it. And it is difficult to keep these things secret because of the constant snooping of neighbors, colleagues, and government functionaries.

Owning a car would, of course, draw attention to me. But I could say, like many of my fellow teachers, I had been on a waiting list (as a World War II veteran, I only had to wait two years, not the usual six); easier to explain than suddenly acquiring large amounts of cash. The car, I reckoned, was better than putting money in the bank.

It was a Lada, and not at all efficient. The East Germans made Trabants, and believe it or not, they are much better than any Lada the Russians ever built.

The biggest problem with the car is that I can't drive it. Since I am a teacher and a veteran, I can get free lessons. My instructor and I found a large plaza and I began to learn the intricacies of the stick shift, changing gears, making turns, and going and stopping. [It must be remembered that Joseph is now in his forties]. Within a week my instructor thought I was ready for a solo.

Everything would probably have gone just fine, except that directly adjoining the plaza was a cemetery. I started my car and drove. Suddenly a funeral truck with a coffin and stools on each side of it where the bereaved sat, loomed in the distance. My intention was to hit the brake, to slow down, but in my confusion I plunged my foot into the accelerator. The truck driver saw what was about to happen, and he slammed his own brakes so hard that the mourners were thrown off entirely and the coffin itself broke the back window and crashed into the cab.

My Lada was badly damaged, with one whole fender and the entire grill, including the radiator, gone, and I didn't want to face Ida and tell her that I had destroyed our immigration money.

First, I told Ida that I would be away for a week or so, in the mountains. Actually, I did still spend some time every year instructing mountain guides, so my message to Ida was not all that strange.

Through a friend I found a mechanic who offered to restore my car, but at a costly price. I worked incognito at the Minsk railroad station, unloading lumber and sand from arriving trains until I had the money to repair my car.

While he waited for the renewal of the five-year contract he was sure he would get, especially because of such good grades at the re-certification school, he was totally unaware of one more thing about the official Soviet line. While the USSR made it appear to the outside world, not the least to the USA, that it had greatly liberalized its immigration policies, it never did tell the representatives of the countries of the world what it did to the relatives, either by blood or marriage, who were left behind.

Shortly after Ida's family left, Joseph confidently faced his fifth contract at Minsk Polytechnic. Excepting the two bigots who had teased him about his Jewishness, he felt "safe." He knew he had the support of most of his colleagues.

He did not know, and neither did the outside world, that the families of those who immigrated either to Israel or to the United States were ultimately put under the most-grave suspicions. And given the paranoid character of the Soviet government at that time, just about anything could happen. This was a fact of life that Joseph and his family learned all too soon.

There was a covert policy to rid all public institutions, including colleges, universities, and polytechnic institutes of any Jew whose family had immigrated to Israel or the United States.

Thus when Joseph came up for re-certification, he did not know that there was an official of the Communist party in attendance. His department chair and his colleagues spoke at length about Joseph's qualifications for continuance. The gist of their testimony was that Joseph was a good man, one who had won teaching awards, who had published in prestigious science journals, and therefore deserved to have his contract renewed.

But then the local Communist stood up and said, in effect, that Joseph could not be renewed for another five years. The functionary called Joseph a bad teacher, and said that his research did not have any real merit.

When the Communist finished, some of Joseph's colleagues endeavored to defend him, but it became increasingly clear that most of them, including his own department head, were backing away from him. They feared Communist party inspired repercussions. They were willing to support Joseph as long as their own jobs were not jeopardized.

Under the watchful eye of the Communist party official, the department took a vote on whether or not to continue Dr. Joseph Gavi on their staff. One by one they voted NO! The vote meant that Joseph would be able to complete the school year at Minsk Polytechnic, but then he would be without a job.

As it turned out, the departmental vote was not the final verdict. There was a committee of thirty to forty people within the Institute – from all departments – who constituted what amounted to an appeals committee. They were the highest professors in the entire institution, and they were supposed to go over everything that might be of benefit to someone who appealed their case to them: teaching abilities, research activities, public service – everything – the whole bit.

JOSEPH   I speak to the committee. I am teaching here for seventeen years. I start to work here in 1956 as a part time teacher, and in 1961, I become full time. I write a dissertation and earn my doctorate. I have numerous publications and teacher awards. I do not understand why I am being fired? What have I done? Is it my fault? Is it because I am a Jew?

And the committee met him with stony silence. No one would tell him – dared tell him – that it was the judgement of the local Communist party that he should be released. Why? Because he was a Jew and because many in his wife's family had left the country. His academic colleagues did not have the heart or the fortitude to help him. Even his department head, who had always been friendly in the past, now spoke out against him, and Joseph knew he did not have a chance.

This was it! Joseph Gavi could stay on at the Institute until late summer, but after that, he would be out of a job. Thus began what undoubtedly was the darkest time of Joseph Gavi's life in the post World War II Soviet Union.

CHAPTER SEVEN

THINKING AMERICAN

He started looking for another teaching job, but was too well known in higher education circles in Minsk to try for an appointment at another university or institution of higher education. Thus, he went to high, junior, and elementary schools.

"What is your previous job?" was always the first question.

"A senior educator at the Polytechnic Institute," he always answered, for it would have been a serious crime, easily detected, if he lied about his past.

"Then, why did you quit there? We certainly cannot offer you in pay or fringe benefits what you get there."

JOSEPH   I am required by law to show my prospective employers my working book, or, as it is frequently called, union book. This is a record of my entire teaching career: when I started to work, teaching awards, recommendations, the entire story of my teaching life, all twenty-four years of it. The book also included the information that I was fired, but of course, it did not state the reasons.

That I was fired because I am a Jew and because Ida's family had immigrated was not listed; I am fired simply for 'incompetence.' Even if these matters had been mentioned in the union book, they would have made no difference to the personnel directors of the public school systems. Indeed, these statistics could make no difference to them: if they hired me, they themselves would stand a good chance of being fired.

Some did ask: "Joseph, why were you released from the Institute?"

"I don't know, I really don't know," I always had to answer.

Joseph considered: "All right, I cannot use my diploma and my educational background any more to have a job. I have worked with my hands before, as a laborer."

He went to a factory, where many of the same old questions dogged him.

"What is your education?"

"I finished high school, and university, and I wrote a dissertation; I have a doctor's degree."

Naively, Joseph thought that the more education he had, the better he could find work. But it did not turn out that way.

JOSEPH "No, no," the personnel manager fairly shouted at me. "We cannot give you a simple labor job. You are over educated. And besides, don't you know that it is forbidden by law to be a laborer with an advanced education?" Ah yes, the law. Always the law.

And it was the same everywhere he went. He could not even find a floor-sweeping job, even with all the medals, ribbons, and diplomas he possessed. He tried many places over several weeks and always came up with nothing.

How in the name of common sense could he provide for his family under these circumstances? By the law, if he stayed unemployed, he would have to go to jail or be kicked out of Minsk to some other part of the Soviet Union – possibly a gulag. In either case, he would have to leave his wife and two children behind, although both Isaac and Alex were now adults, to fend for themselves. At no cost would he voluntarily split up his family.

Joseph and Ida and the two boys did benefit somewhat from several parcels sent to them from Miami by Ida's sister, Fania. They were packed full of jeans and shirts and other types of clothing. Whenever Joseph went to the post office to receive a parcel, he had to fill out a form attesting that he would not sell them on the thriving Soviet black market. In every instance, though, he broke the law. He sold all these things, because his family needed the money.

To supplement these meager cash reserves, Joseph began operating a "jitney" service with his Lada, completely illegal in the tightly controlled Soviet Union cab industry. "There were, however, not enough government owned taxis, and everybody was always looking for a ride." He was paid in cash for his services – never charging more than the government rate – and soon he had a small clientele of satisfied customers. Unsuspectingly, perhaps, he was already on his way to becoming a capitalist.

Then, too, with his Lada, he could crash the vegetable market in Ukraine. In June – the month he was fired – vegetables became scarce in Minsk. He knew that if he went to Ukraine, the "bread basket of the Soviet Union," he could get a carload of tomatoes, and perhaps obtain a fine price for them on the Minsk market. Again, illegal to be sure, but he had to do something.

He and Alex drove out of Minsk and passed all the checkpoint inspections without incident. They went on to Kiev and Joseph bought two hundred pounds of tomatoes, and stowed them away in the trunk and backseat, camouflaging them as best he could. He knew he could get a long prison sentence if he were caught, and, for that matter, so could Alex.

JOSEPH   As we approach Minsk, we come to a large roadblock, and I begin to worry. How am I going to get this load through? I know they would look into the car and, as was sometimes the case, search it from top to bottom. I am prepared to make a run for it if I have to, and in preparation, I stop well before the checkpoint and take off my license plates.

As it happens, there is a big line at the checkpoint, overworking the guards. Each driver rolls up to the waiting policemen who either slightly or thoroughly check his vehicle, and then drive off as quickly as possible, to have this ordeal behind him.

I spot a large semi, eighteen-wheeler in the line. I drive up on its right side. Each time it stops, I stop. The semi driver knows what I am up to and, in fact, starts to whistle loudly when he stops to show his papers to the waiting policemen. If the lawmen were to look through the semi's wheels, they would see me and Alex on the other side. But they are apparently impressed by the cheerful truck driver, and bid him a good journey. On the other side of the truck, I also speed up. After a short time of paralleling the truck further, I gun my accelerator as much as the little Lada will take, wave an affectionate farewell to my benefactor, and head straight for Minsk. There, I find a lady who runs an impromptu market and I sell my tomatoes to her.

We – Alex and I – made good money on our adventure to Kiev, but I decided not repeat it. Too risky, I thought. I heard later that while my tomatoes were being sold, a policeman came by and demanded that the lady tell him where they came from. "I could confiscate the lot," the policeman said, "or destroy them right here." I heard, though, that he wound up buying a goodly supply of tomatoes for himself and family.

A couple of months after getting the vegetables, a Soviet authority asked Joseph the question he had been dreading: "How and where are you getting enough money to pay your rent each month? And to buy food?" There was no choice but for Joseph to tell the truth.

"You will now be prosecuted as a traitor," he was told. Ironic, this, he thought, in view of his services to his country during the war. And his youngest son would be affected. Isaac had just completed his degree; he was now twenty-three, and married.

But Alex was just eighteen, and he would lose his status as a student.

One day in a deep depression, Joseph came home and told Ida, "Enough is enough. We are going to immigrate." And this statement began another intensely dramatic and difficult aspect of the Gavi family's lives.

He filled out an application, and named his wife Ida, his son Isaac and daughter-in-law, Zina, and son Alex as those who would accompany him. His destination? Israel, of course.

In the mid 1970s the Soviet government began to ease up on granting exit visas to those Jews who wished to travel to Israel and even the United States, all in the name of "family reunification." Much of the western world, including the United States, hailed the Soviet Union's new "liberal" policies.

In 1973, for example, 34,922 Soviet Jews left the USSR; in 1974, 20,181 received visa exits. The number dropped in 1975 to 13,189; and increased somewhat for 1976, up to 14,178.[28] In 1977, some 16,736 left the country. In the early part of 1978, it appeared that "emigration had reached a plateau." But, suddenly in June, the number of exit visas rose sharply.

Good relations between China and the United States rose in that year, too, and the Salt II agreements seemed to be an indication of rapprochement between the US and the USSR.[29] Altogether, in 1978, the year Joseph Gavi and his family emigrated, 28,865 Jews left the Soviet Union, and it seems clear that if relationships between the United States and the Soviet Union had not been in a state of improvement, this would not have happened. (But this year, 1978, was by no means the high water mark in Soviet emigration. Just the next year, 1979, an astounding 51,333 left the Soviet Union. Certainly a part of this giant number had to do with trying to get goodwill around the world because the World Olympics were scheduled for Moscow in 1980).[30]

Toward those Soviet Jews who expressed a wish to leave the country, the government was anything but liberal. In early January 1978 six prominent Jews wrote to President Jimmy Carter, telling him that not all was as he imagined it to be in the Soviet Union in reference to Jews. "There are no signs so far of a change in the emigration policy of the USSR," they wrote, "and during the last year the persecution of Jews wishing to leave… has been especially intensified."[31] Signed by mathematicians Solomon Alber, Viktor Brailovsky, Aleksandr Lerner and Naum Melman, and physicists Yakov Albert and Yuri Golfand, the letter said that "official and anti-Semitic propaganda" had increased in the Soviet press, with Jewish activists accused of being spies."[32] Apparently, President Carter did not respond to this letter.

In June the Soviet authorities filed criminal charges against two Jewish dissidents, Vladimir and Mariya Slepak. They had unfurled a large banner from the balcony of their Moscow apartment saying, "Let Us Out To Our Son in Israel."[33] Also in June ten Soviet Jews were held for protesting government visa policy. They gathered outside the Secret Police headquarters and chanted and yelled epithets at the authorities.[34] On the whole, 1978

---

[28] The New York Times, 22 January 1978.

[29] These statistics come from Howard M. Sachar, Diaspora: An Inquiry Into the Contemporary World, 1985), 452-455.

[30] Ibid.

[31] The New York Times, 22 January 1978.

[32] Ibid.

[33] Ibid. 4 June 1978.

[34] Ibid. 10 June 1978.

was not exactly the most efficacious year Joseph Gavi could have picked for leaving the country.

Was Joseph harassed for applying for a visa? Not exactly – at least at the beginning of the process. In fact, after a few days without hearing or seeing anything unusual, Joseph began to hope that he would be left alone. Zina's (Isaac's wife) mother strongly opposed her leaving the country, for not only familial reasons but patriotic as well. Her father, however, approved, believing her life would be better elsewhere. He asked Ida to be Zina's "mother" in the difficult weeks and months that lay ahead.

Joseph was somewhat concerned that his low-level security clearances of a few years before would cause the authorities to keep him from leaving. He really had no military secrets, however, and thus made no mention of the expedition to the Pamirs, hoping that the officials would not find about it. They either did not discover it, or it made no difference to them.

Of far greater importance than security clearances was what now happened to Alex. Joseph came home one day to find a tearful family; Alex had received his draft notice. He was to report immediately to the military authorities.

The last thing in the world Joseph wanted was to split up his immediate family. By now Rachel was deceased and his brother, Leva, had his own family in Minsk. But to leave his beloved younger son behind? The thought was unacceptable.[35]

After Alex reported, he went through the usual routines of recruits everywhere: batteries of medical examinations and a very short haircut.

While Alex did all this, Joseph went directly to the military recruiting officer.

JOSEPH   "I have filled out all the documents for my family and me to leave the country for good. Why are you doing this to us? You know that, officially, I and all my family have now been declared traitors to the Soviet Union just because we want to immigrate to Israel. How can you take him into the army under these circumstance?"

"We know you are going to Israel," the colonel told me. "Israel needs soldiers and in three years time, after Alex Gavi has served in our army, Israel can have a fully trained soldier. He will

---

[35] Rachel died in 1973. Just before her death, she expressed to Joseph her wish that he would quit smoking, and in her honor and at her funeral, Joseph vowed to do so. He smoked for thirty years, even while climbing in the rarefied atmosphere of the mountains. He had smoked a "paperose," a cigarette with a pipe-like stem in it, with tobacco held at a constant distance from his mouth. He has not touched anything with nicotine in it since 1973.

have all the experience Israel needs in a soldier." The colonel was actually taunting me as he gave me this information.

There is no way I will immigrate either to Israel or the United States without Alex. Beyond our love for Alex, there is the danger to me and Ida and Isaac if Alex stays behind. He can very well become a hostage in the Soviet Union. They can blackmail us. Make us do things to keep Alex safe. Even become spies for the Soviet Union. If they have our son in their grasp, they can do almost anything to us.

Joseph and Ida decided that twenty-three year old Isaac and his wife, Zina, would go on ahead of them. They knew that relatives in the United States would help Isaac and his pregnant wife, but still "it broke our heart," that now, despite our best efforts, the family would have to be split up. "It was a terrible, terrible time for us. I was full of worry and bitterness."

Joseph and Ida went with Alex on the day he was to be inducted into the army. He had to line up with some forty other young men, and then the colonel started a roll call. He did not, however, call out Alex's name, and Joseph had a momentary quickening of his body. Maybe, just maybe, he thought to himself, God has listened to our prayers.

After the roll call, the colonel motioned to Joseph.

"Mr. Gavi, please accompany me to my office." Now I began to worry about some other kind of unpleasant surprise. Ida and I followed the colonel to his office.

JOSEPH   "Mr. Gavi, because you have decided to be a traitor to your country, I am afraid your son is a traitor also. And we cannot have traitors in the Soviet army. Go home, and take your precious immigration."

On the one hand, these were harsh words, hard to take. I am an honored Soviet veteran from World War II. I am by no means a traitor to my country, and would like to have told the arrogant colonel that it was the anti-Jewish policies of my own country that were forcing me to leave.

On the other hand, I have Alex back, and for that I am immeasurably grateful. Ida and I and Alex, all three now in tears of both frustration and happiness, hurry back to our own apartment. The colonel, in a very important way, is unwittingly making it easier for me to leave my native country.

Joseph's immigration papers had been filed, and Alex was now as safe as could be expected under the circumstances. If his immigration application were accepted, he would be happy, but at the same time he knew there would be much governmental bureaucracy to overcome. If the application were not accepted, he would be branded as a "refusenik," and be forever without a job and forced into abject poverty. He would be endlessly persecuted by the authorities for being a "traitor," and there would be no one to whom he could appeal.

In the meantime, however, he kept receiving "care" packages from the States. He could not now sell the jeans and other clothing to "secondary" stores, because he was too much under Soviet surveillance. So he continued the illegal and dangerous black market, selling on the streets.

Joseph had heard that it took about two months for the Soviet bureaucrats to process an application for an exit visa. But two months passed, and more, and Joseph heard nothing.

Thus, he began going to the Soviet visa office in Minsk to keep a constant check on his status. At least on one occasion, his visit ended in a shouting match. "Don't bother us with your stupid questions!" he was told. "You will know when or if your exit visa application has been approved!"

Joseph thought: "When you are so insecure, and you have a family to care for, you can't sleep at nights. When will it be? Tomorrow? This week? Next week? Next month? Never?" He couldn't abide the silence, and he decided to be bold about it. Whatever else happened, Dr. Joseph Gavi was not going to stand around and be ignored.

JOSEPH   There is always such a long line at the visa office that I go there at 5:00 a.m., only to find that some of the other thousands who want to immigrate have begun their stay in line at midnight or at the latest at two in the morning. Everyone is given a number, and for several mornings, I simply did not make it before the office closed down for the day.

Finally, though, my time comes. "What is happening with my papers?" I asked loudly; I am afraid, very loudly. The functionary behind the counter shuffles some documents for a few minutes and looks seriously into several folders. "Gavi. Gavi." he repeats. "What do we have?"

Then the clerk looks straight into my face and says, "yes, yes, we have the application, but nothing has happened yet. Go home and wait. Don't keep bothering us." I stared at the flunkie and said angrily, "Yes I will go home."

In a depressed mood I go home. When I get there, the first thing I see is a letter in my post box from the same office I have just visited. It said, "yes, it is all right for you to immigrate. Your request for an exit visa has been approved."

That son-of-a-bitch! He knows when I saw him that my application has been approved by the higher authorities. He simply wants me to suffer for another three or four hours. The son-of-a-bitch! I cannot find words to describe my feelings. It is everything to put you down until the last second, to make you think your application will not be approved. The truth is that the bureaucrats know we are leaving, and that beyond the borders of the Soviet Union, we will be free people. Are the bureaucrats jealous? They must be!

The next day Joseph was in line again, armed with the letter he had received the day before, this time to get his official approval to leave the Soviet Union. The sanctioned paper said that Joseph and his family had thirty days to clear up all their liabilities, private and to the government, before they could leave.

And what did Joseph and his family have to do during this one-month period?

First came a full re-modeling of their apartment, plus a completely new coating of paint. Why did they do this? Because the authorities ordered it. The apartment had to be in "tip-top" shape for the next occupants, perhaps occupants who were not inclined to "desert" Mother Russia.

The whole family had to retrieve their birth certificates. In some instances the records had been kept so shoddily or ignored altogether during the war that this was a difficult process.

Then they must order their railroad tickets to get them out of the country. If you had any baggage (which most assuredly they did, which included a few books, Joseph's medals and ribbons from the war, many family photographs, especially from the mountains, and his scientific articles), you have to take it to Brest-Litovsk for shipments to your most immediate European destination, which, in this case, was Vienna.

At first he was told by the authorities, "No, you cannot ship any books," and he had resorted to shipping out packages to Vienna, care of the Hebrew Immigration Aid Society (HIAS), his sponsor out of Russia, a few books at a time. And, in one of these packages of books, he secreted his doctoral dissertation. Legally, he was not supposed to do this. The authorities did not want anyone in Israel or the United States to know that their new arrival was an accomplished intellectual. The dissertation arrived, because the customs people in Russia were apparently more interested in finding out whether or not the Gavis were smuggling silver or gold out of the country than in academic achievements.

And, of course, they had to sell their Lada. This turned out, actually, to be the easiest part of the whole ordeal. Isaac had a friend whose uncle in Leningrad was a butcher, a "money-making" profession in the Soviet Union at that time, especially given all the opportunities to sell meat on the blackmarket.

Though he could have afforded it, the Leningrad butcher did not wish to buy a new car. Why? Because it would have brought bureaucratic and police attention to him. They would eventually have asked him: "How is it that you have an 'official' salary of eighty rubles a month and you are buying a car that costs ten to twelve thousand rubles?" It would have been an endless matter of bribing the police to get them to leave him alone.

The un-named butcher heard about Joseph's car. He flew up to Minsk one morning, bringing a suitcase of money – it appeared to Joseph to be some twenty thousand rubles. Joseph paid six thousand rubles for the Lada, and he would have been embarrassed to ask the butcher for more. Even after he had re-decorated and re-furnished their apartment, he still had a few thousand rubles left over.

The butcher gave Joseph six thousand rubles for the car, and paid another thousand to a clerk in the Minsk motor department for a quick transfer of title. He drove the car back to Leningrad that very afternoon.

It turned out that there were so many things for Joseph, Ida, Isaac and Zina, and Alex to do that they could not meet the thirty-day deadline to leave. "There were so many thousands of people leaving the Soviet Union in 1978," Joseph recalls, "that there just simply was not enough time to do everything by way of preparation." He had to apply for a one-week extension, which was grudgingly granted by the authorities.

And by now, there weren't just five of them. In one way of looking at it, there were six. Back in 1972, Isaac had dreamed of owning his own dog, and he approached Joseph with the idea. "I didn't make enough money to feed my family," Joseph said, "let alone a dog."[36]

Joseph kept putting Isaac off, but one day told him that if he were accepted as a student into Minsk Polytechnic, he would buy him a dog. Even though at that time Joseph still taught at the Institute, he was not at all convinced that Isaac could be enrolled because of the family's Jewishness.

But Isaac was accepted, and soon after the Gavis had visited a dog club. There they found a nice German shepherd. They bought him and named him Amer. Had the name been a subconscious desire by the family? Much of Ida's family, as we have seen, had already been to America, and perhaps that was why the dog became Amer. But it could have been an unexpressed wish to go to America themselves.

JOSEPH The family took much pride in Amer, giving him as best we could obedience training. He was such a nice dog, everybody loved him. He was just like a human being. But he also grew to a large size.

When we first began to make specific plans to immigrate, we and the family conceded that Amer would have to be left behind. But as departure day neared, the thought became unbearable. The day before we left the Soviet Union for good, we expressed the thought that we could at least get Amer as far as Vienna and then decide from there what to do with him.

I learned, almost at the last moment, through the Hebrew Aid Immigration Aid Society that I could take Amer with me to Austria. So, on the very day we left – Ida and I, our son Isaac and his wife, Zina, and our son, Alex – along with us was a tail-wagging German shepherd named Amer.

And so, finally, the Gavi family, in tears and wonderment, made final their plans to leave the land of their birth. They were like thousands of their compatriots. They wanted to leave for a life where Jewishness would not constantly be an object of scorn. But then, the Soviet Union was their Motherland, and all of them – especially Joseph, with his ghetto and partisan work in World War II – had mixed feelings about leaving. They all realized now the phenomenon of being happy and sad at the same time.

The night before the Gavis left, there was a loud knocking on their door, and with some trepidation – "what could the authorities want now?" crossed his mind – Joseph answered it. No chairs or tables were left in the

---

[36] Today, in Louisville, Kentucky, Joseph says: "With my 5,000 square feet home, I can have all the dogs I want!"

house; just the family, with bare floor space. It was, thankfully, not the KGB telling him he could not go to America after all, as he feared, but a friend, a fellow mountain climber, an Armenian named Ruben Arutunian.

He stood in the doorway with large loaves of bread, salami, and a "huge" bottle of cognac. Before anyone, Joseph or Ruben or the rest of Joseph's family could say anything, everyone broke down in tears.

JOSEPH He was not a rich man. He was a factory worker who received a small salary. Yet he bought a ticket – not cheap – all the way from Armenia to Minsk to see us before our departure! He was such a good friend!

When I could speak, I asked Ruben, "why do you do this?"

"Because we are friends, and this may be the last time we'll ever see each other."

Ruben passed out the bread and salami and uncorked the cognac and, though our train was leaving early, we had a feast that lasted until well into the morning.

Even the next day Ruben would not part from Joseph. He got into the train with Joseph, Ida, Zina and Isaac, Alex, and Amer, and went with them as far as he could within the Soviet Union; that is, Brest-Litovsk. The ride was about six and a half hours, and it was a poignant, bittersweet experience for them all. (Joseph has not seen Ruben since that day, though he has corresponded with him. While Joseph was in Rome, waiting to be transported to the United States, he sent a large package of clothes to Ruben and his family).

The train from Brest-Litovsk through Poland was so crowded that there was hardly any place to sit, let alone lie down. Amer stayed on the floor, under the lowest bunk, so scared that he was shaking. Zina, being pregnant, got the first bunk, and Isaac, Alex, and Joseph and Ida divided up the rest as best they could.

They soon fell into a fitful sleep, so it was not difficult for them to awaken at daylight to the sound of harsh knocking on their compartment door. They did not know exactly where they were, but they guessed they should be coming into Czechoslovakia. Still, they could yet be in Poland and their chances of being taken back to Minsk – for whatever reasons the authorities might concoct – were, to them, quite realistic.

The knocking continued, but the Gavi family did not respond. Finally, the train conductor took his own keys and hurriedly, and rather angrily, opened the door himself. He did not tarry, because a snarling, snapping Amer came straight for him. He judiciously closed the door just in time to save himself from canine wrath. At that point, Joseph was grateful that they had brought Amer with them.

Another scare was in store for them:

JOSEPH Entering Austria at 5:00 a.m. four men entered our car, all armed with machine guns. Again, Amer tried to charge them, but I stayed him because I feared one of the men would shoot him. It was only later that we learned that these men were our 'friends.' They were actually inspecting the entire train for infiltrators from the Palestine Liberation Organization. (When I first heard of the PLO, I was positively impressed. How can an organization that fights for 'liberation' be less than great)?

Apparently, when the PLO learned of a train coming from Russia through Poland and Czechoslovakia to Austria, they would frequently try to waylay it, to prevent one more Jew from ever reaching Israel.

At this point in the journey, from an official point of view, everyone was still going to Israel; only in Vienna would the Gavis – and thousands of others – declare their intent to go the United States. The guards, then, were numerous and alert, but at the same time, they were frightening to Joseph Gavi and his family, all trying their best to change their status from "comrade" to "citizen."

CHAPTER EIGHT

BECOMING AMERICAN

A rriving at the big train station in Vienna there were two lines for Soviet refugees. In one line were buses and, as Ida said, "people just disappeared into them." These were the emigres going directly to Israel. In fact, the very next day, they were all flown directly to Tel Aviv. But for the rest, and this included the Gavi family, there were vans to take the "other options" (which usually meant Canada or the USA) to various places in the Austrian city. Many of the van drivers by-passed the Gavis, in part, apparently, because they feared a confrontation with Amer. Joseph hung a medal around Amer's neck to show that he was well behaved and would obey his owner. They finally got a ride.

In Vienna, they were lodged by the Hebrew Immigration Aid Society, in a small apartment, near Strauss Park, all six of them in one room. One of the first things they did upon arrival in Vienna was to telephone a friend (somewhat dangerous for the friend) in Minsk to see if they had received any late arriving mail. Yes they had.

The letter they received in Minsk from HIAS in Vienna told the Gavis that if they decided to go to the US they could not take Amer with them from Vienna to Rome, the embarkation place for American sojourners. They confirmed this information with the local HIAS, so they set about getting their beloved Amer out of the country. They contacted Ida's brother-in-law, Valery, in Chicago, and he promised to receive the dog if they had to "mail" him.

Now, from Vienna, the Gavis had the choice of either selling Amer or sending him away. They, of course, decided on the latter.

First, they had to have a wooden cage built that would adequately house the large dog. While Joseph led Amer to the shop for measurements, a policeman stopped him and offered to buy the dog. He said he would give a few thousand shillings for him. Amer was from good breeding, and had won some some citations and medals at shows and would, in all probability, continue to do the same for the Vienna officer.

JOSEPH   It would be like selling a member of the family, I told the man. There is no question of our parting with Amer. There can't be.

We took Amer and his cage to the airport, where a veterinarian gave him a shot against the rabies, and pronounced the dog fit to travel, and to be accepted in the host country.

The entire Gavi family, all of us, myself, Ida, Isaac and Zina, and Alex, were in tears. It was so terrible. Here was our good friend being sent away from us, perhaps forever. The incident turned out happily. We later found Amer waiting for us in Chicago.

Joseph could afford to send Amer to Chicago because of the "immigration money" that Sima had given him and Ida, of which some was left, his meager savings, and HIAS advancements.

Meanwhile, in Vienna, they had to survive. They had been allowed only a small amount of money out of Minsk, and then the cost of sending Amer to the States, definitely did make a dent in the meager finanical resources.

JOSEPH   We had enough money for bread and tomatoes, and chicken, because chicken in Vienna is so cheap, unlike beef, which is dear. We had a little pot (no oven) in our hotel room, but it was not big enough to cook a whole chicken. So, when we bought a chicken, we cut it in half and cooked it. We did have a little electric coil to make chicken soup. So, for the most part in Vienna, it was bread, tomatoes, and chicken, chicken, chicken!

(Perhaps he and Ida were unconsciously and unwittingly preparing themselves for one of their most noted dishes in Louisville, Kentucky).

JOSEPH But it was always better than anything we had ever had back in Minsk.

Wandering around Vienna, the Byelorussian family was thoroughly fascinated by the sights. The abundance of fruits and vegetables they had not seen since their trip to Tashkent several years before. St. Stephen's Cathedral, the Votary Church, the museums, the Stables of the Lippazaners, the opera, and the houses of the great virtuosos – it was really too much!

How could people live like this in Vienna and people live like that in Minsk, not actually all that far away? Surely, something is wrong with the world's economy to make people in the former so much better off socially, economically, and politically than in the latter. It was definitely something for the Gavi family, still suffering the pangs of departure from their native land, to ponder.

They especially had to be careful of money because Zina was pregnant and she had to use bathrooms more often than other members of the family. "If you use bathrooms in Vienna," Ida wistfully recalls, "you have to pay the money."

JOSEPH After some ten days in Vienna HIAS representatives came to visit us in our hotel room. "Where do you intend to go?" they asked, "Israel or the United States?"

It took me about ten seconds to reply:

"The United States."

And that, of course, had been our decision all along. We just could not make it 'official' until this moment.

And so, because we have now opted for America, this means we have to travel from Vienna to Rome, to undergo additional tests and orientations, and obtain entry visas.

On the train from Vienna to Rome, machine-gun toting, very hefty, men were hired – Joseph reckoned them to be from the Mafia – to guard them. There were some 200 Soviet Jews on the train who had opted for the United States, and the threat of a PLO retaliation was quite realistic. About forty miles before they got to Rome, the train stopped and everyone was ordered onto buses. Still with escorts armed with machine guns, the buses proceeded into Rome, precisely to the places that had been pre-scheduled by HIAS for these refugees to stay, to avoid interference by unfriendly groups.

Actually, the family could have immigrated somewhat more quickly than they did had it not been for Zina's pregnancy. Pan American Airlines would not take them, because their directors were afraid that Zina would give birth during flight, and they would not know what to do. Of course, Joseph and Ida and Alex could have gone on before, and left Isaac and Zina behind. But they were family. And they meant to stay together.

But Rome was absolutely wonderful and enchanting to the traveling family. They thought they had immersed themselves into the western world by their stay in Vienna; but they had not yet been to Rome.

Ostia, Rome's ancient and historic seaport, had a "Fascist" section where middle-class people lived in fairly expensive apartments. Another part was the "Communist" section, where the relatively poor resided. Joseph and his family took up residence in this latter area.

In a way, it was like getting a three month subsidized vacation while waiting for Zina to give birth to Joseph's and Ida's first grandchild. HIAS gave just enough money for the rent and food.

JOSEPH   Each morning I bought a large loaf of bread for the family, and a gallon of wine for thirty cents – we had, most definitely, been told not to 'drink the water' – at a 'specialty store,' where in one big room there were literally dozens of barrels of wine, from floor to ceiling. All you had to do was open up the faucet on a barrel and let the wine pour.

I usually brought two buckets with me. No one ever got drunk – certainly not me; I remembered my navy days – but we were never thirsty either. We were two hundred yards from the sea, and we frolicked in it almost every day, and I played chess with the numerous men and boys who set up tables along the boardwalk.

In Ostia one day Ida and I came upon a meat market, and saw a large plate of liver in the display case. I wanted some liver, as long as it was beef and not pork. We differed – my wife and I – on the appearance, and actually got into a quarrel about whether it was pork or beef. Finally the proprietor showed up, and I put pointed fingers to my forehead, as though they were horns, and shouted or, actually asked, "moo-moo?"

Sadly, at least for me, the store owner answered back, "oink-oink."

Nevertheless, the two Russian expatriates who did not know the Italian language, provided a humorous diversions for onlookers and passers-by.

Although Isaac did have to take a job as a HIAS guard to supplement their family's income, they frequently went to downtown Rome, some twenty miles away, and visited cathedrals and, of course, the coliseum. Whenever historical events and personalities were explained by head-telephones, they always selected English, and this way picked up their first words and phrases in the language. They also patronized the Gogol Library, which had books useful for bridging the gap between Russian and English. They went often to the Formicino Flea Market, said to be world's largest and oldest and reportedly run by the Mafia, where they bought needed household goods.

The good times, though, were conditioned by worrisome thoughts:

JOSEPH   How is everything going to be once we get to our final destination, and try to settle in? I kept asking myself. We were heading ultimately for Chicago, because that is where Valery and Alla live, and of great importance to us, where Amer has been sent. I have no money beyond a certain point.

And, I have no language. Without the English language, I cannot achieve any level of society. I knew I would have to work as a laborer until I could read and write some English. No matter: I had spent much time in hard labor before – but that was as a young man – I was confident, though, that I could do it again. The price was not too great.

All these thoughts were pushed aside one day when Zina called out to the rest of the family: "The baby's coming!"

Isaac ran into a street and stopped a taxi, and shouted "Bambino! Bambino!"

The perplexed cabbie kept looking around for a child, as Isaac continued to yell "Bambino! Bambino!" Finally, Joseph and Ida got Zina out to the street, and the taxi driver understood at once what was happening, and rushed the couple to a hospital in Rome.

Isaac waited "forever" in that hospital. He could not understand anyone, and they could not understand him. Finally, though, a nurse did make Isaac know that he had just become a father.

Elated, Isaac dialed the apartment building's common telephone and was finally able to tell Joseph and Ida:"We have a baby. It is a boy. His name is David."

Joseph exulted. "Now instead of a dog, we have a child!"

Back at their apartment, however, a problem arose. They had signed an agreement – only half understood – with their landlady that no children would live with them, even though the landlady could very well see and know Zina's condition. No other apartment was available that Joseph could afford, not with some 55,000 other immigrants looking for homes as well.

In violation of the lease, they brought David home with them. Three other immigrant families lived in the same building, and they worked out a plan with the Gavis to keep David's presence a secret. During the landlady's frequent inspections, a neighbor took David onto the balcony. Another time, a visiting friend went from one room to another with David, leaving just before the woman entered. Fortunately, David did not cry on these occasions.

JOSEPH   During our last days in Ostia, when David was about a month old, we learned that all of this subterfuge was not even necessary. The landlady caught us with David – maybe she knew all along – and she turned out to be kindly. "Why didn't you tell me? I would not have thrown you out! Not at all! Not with a little baby!"

The incident put me in mind of perhaps once again trusting people – looking for their better instincts. But I had had too many experiences of governmental and bureaucratic harassment; it would take a long time – if ever – for me to be comfortable with authority.

Finally, our day of departure was at hand. We were informed by HIAS to prepare for a 25 July 1978 flight on Pan American Airways. We are ready! I exclaimed to them and to anybody around me. Only two suitcases for all of us!

As the plane lifted off from Leonardo da Vinci Airport, Joseph's mood was exultant, but mixed with poignancy. Ida was in tears, but "anxious to leave." She wanted to re-establish her's and Joseph's lives. "The thought that we did not belong to anyone," she says, "was disturbing." They no longer were bound to the Soviet Union; they did not yet "belong" to the United States. Thus, they were in limbo. Yes, they were "free," but literally at this point of Pan Am's takeoff, they were people without a country, and it did not set well with them. "One who has never experienced the feeling," Ida said, "cannot understand our thoughts at that moment." Nevertheless, they both sensed that they were leaving the Old World forever. They had ceased being "Comrades;" now they must put their energies toward becoming "Citizens."

The flight was uneventful – at least until they got to JFK, the port of entry on the way to Chicago.

JOSEPH   Even while in the air I noted that the automobiles in New York are as big as Soviet train cars. A HIAS representative met us and issued White Cards, so we could have permanent residence, and took us to a hotel, and this gave me my second great discovery, (beyond the cars). It was really the first time I had ever slept in a real bed. [He was now 47 years old] In Vienna and Ostia the entire family was in one room, and so I slept on the floor. In Russia Ida and I had never had a bed – just a matress or foldaway cot. But here, at the New York hotel the bed was so big that I could lie this way or that way, either vertically or horizontally. [But one must remember that Joseph is barely five feet tall].

The whole family is astonished at how long a hot shower we can take here. "You can stay under the water as long as you want," I exulted. In Minsk, bathing facilities had been primitive, and not much better in Vienna where we shared facilities with several families, and in Rome where we had to put money into an electric meter to get hot water. Here in New York it is wonderful! Such small things! But so important!

The next morning we flew to Chicago. My first sights of the Windy City – from the air – were of all the spaghetti highways. How in the world, I asked myself, am I ever going to cope with that kind of traffic? Cars are literally going everywhere, and I was not big driver of cars in the first places (remembering my accident with the Lada). I closed my eyes: I cannot look on this. It is too much.

I thought further: If I cannot drive a car, how then will I get a job? And I must have a job for the family to survive. I know that HIAS funds will not last much longer; in fact, the help I received from HIAS was on the premise that I find gainful employment, and ultimately re-pay much of the funds they had advanced me.

My brother-in-law, Valery, met us at O'Hare, and took us to his and Alla's apartment. We were unpleasantly surprised that Amer would have nothing to do with us. After all, we had shipped Amer out of Vienna to 'fend for himself,' or I suppose he thought, and he was angry. It took some time for Amer to be reconciled to the family, especially David, the newcomer.

For a month Joseph and Ida lived with Valery and Alla, while Isaac, Zina, David, and Alex stayed with Ida's brother, Vladimir and his wife Lora, in another part of town. They did not like to separate the family even for this short time, but it was the best they could do. Joseph found an apartment on Lunt Street, near Lakeshore Drive, and so they were together once more, this time including Amer, who ultimately forgave them. They wanted, at all costs, to keep the family unit intact.

Vladimir, Joseph's brother-in-law, was a paint contractor, who employed three or four other painters. The morning after arrival, Joseph went to work for him, jet lag and all, along with Isaac and Alex. At the end of the first week Vladimir handed Joseph a check, covering the wages for all three men.

JOSEPH   I looked at the check and asked Vladimir.

Okay, but where is our money?

Vladimir laughed, and explained.

Still, I was unbelieving, though he was my kinsman. How do I spend it? It is only a piece of paper. Do I cut little pieces from it to pay for whatever it is I buy?

It was all so ironic. Back in the Soviet Union, I was the smart guy. I was the scientist. But I did not know of checking systems.

"Don't worry," Vladimir assured me. "I will get it cashed for you and help you to open a checking account at a bank." And so I was introduced to a very important way of life that I would quickly and happily get used to: Capitalism!

The three worked for $3.50 an hour each. This meant that collectively they made $10.50 hourly. They worked anywhere from forty to sixty hours a week. "We felt like millionaires."

And they needed every cent they earned. They were expected to repay HIAS for the subsidies in Vienna and Ostia, and for the air tickets from Rome to Chicago (dispelling the belief of many Americans that immigrants were always fully subsidized, even by the U.S. government). They immediately began to set aside weekly funds for this purpose. They arrived in America already owing some $8,000 and, and one might say, this was another important lesson in Capitalism that the Gavi family learned early one – that credit is an integral part of the system.

JOSEPH The first major appliance I buy was an upright freezer, because we are shocked at what we could see in supermarkets. Back in Russia, we bought food on a daily basis – whatever we needed for one day – for there was no way of preserving foodstuffs.

At Delmonico's, it was unreal. I could buy chicken twenty five to thirty pounds of it at one time and keep frozen until it was used. I simply could not refuse to buy the beautiful chickens! We were so enchanted with all the fruits, vegetables, and meats that Alex piled a table full of chicken and salami, took a photograph of it and sent it back to Uncle Leva in Minsk – not to mock or taunt – but to induce him to immigrate as well.

[He never did. Both he and his wife are music teachers in Minsk].

(Today, with only a year or so left of the twentieth century, it appears that only the Soviet Union ended, not the tyranny. The presidents of one "Commonwealth" after another have already decreed "emergency powers" by which they can have their own ways over any representative form of government. "Commonwealth" citizens with ties to the New World, particularly the United States, are just as suspect of "spying" as in the old Soviet Union. No reasons are ever given; it is apparently the same old paranoia that so affected the leaders from Moscow in the first place).

JOSEPH Speaking of tyranny, there was one thing in America I simply could not get used to: Chicago policemen. Every time I see one in the distance, I will change to the other side of the street.

For three or four years in Chicago I am scared to talk to anyone, let alone a policeman. Back in Minsk, I have no way of knowing if the person I meet on the street, policeman or not, was to be trusted. Any slip of the tongue or even honest mistake could be reported to the authorities, and what you said, perhaps in all innocence, could be used against you in a court of law.

Our family was counseled by the Jewish Vocational Services in Chicago. On our first trip, I took my diplomas, including the Ph.D, with me. The man at the Services listened while I, through an interpreter, told of my educational accomplishments and experiences. When we finished, the man said to me and Isaac and Alex: "These diplomas will not do anything for you. An education won't feed you. You have to do something with your hands to earn a living."

It was only sometime later that I learned that the counselor's words ran exactly counter to what most immigrants had always believed to be the 'American Dream:' get an education and use it, and you will prosper.

He was an official, and all my life I had had to listen to authority. It was bad advice. Terribly bad advice. I was forty-seven years old, with a doctorate in physiology, along with twenty-nine articles, and many years of teaching experience, and today [the late 90s] I speak seven different languages.

In the Gavi apartment they spoke Byelorussian, to a considerable extent because they wanted David to grow up with the language – exemplifying the old immigrant adage that it was "Europe in the home and America in the streets." They did, however, attend evening English classes, for Joseph knew that if he were going to get any meaningful work, he had to learn English. Isaac did learn English very quickly, and found work with an engineering firm. Alex went to high school in Chicago and learned quickly, too.

JOSEPH   I was all right during the first part of these English learning sessions – which frequently lasted four hours. I have already worked ten to twelve hours as a painter, rising at 5 each day to get to my job. I had never worked physically for so many hours, even when I run the jackhammer in Minsk after the navy. It was too much for me, so I quit the language school. I hope I can learn English some other way.

I could not keep up as a painter. If I had to work on ceilings all day I come home with a fierce headache and agonizing neck muscles, and all I want to do is sleep. I left Vladimir and went to a German constructor. My German was good enough that the boss could not believe I came from Minsk. But then, the recession of the late 1970s began, and I was laid off.

My employer telephoned the chief of the local painters' union and told him: "I'm going to send you an immigrant. He doesn't know the language and he's not much of a painter, but I've done you some favors in the past, and you can now do one for me." I joined the union, and was guaranteed $9.75 an hour for whatever construction-painting-odd job I might perform.

My first job was at the Cook County Jail where, for several weeks, I painted and did odd jobs. [One of the first people he saw at the prison was the notorious serial killer, John Wayne Gacy). On day one, my supervisor began to speak to me in English. This is the end, I thought – in Russian, of course – I don't understand a word he is saying to me. The boss saw my perplexed look, and asked "Do you understand?" "No!" I replied, perhaps a little bit too emphatically.

My chief at the jail was from Poland – and I was fluent in that language. It was just a matter of both of us letting each other know that we spoke a common language. I worked at the jail for a year – until 1980.

He formed many impressions of American life just by working at the Cook County Jail. He noted a familiarity between prisoners and guards that would never have happened in the Soviet Union. At lunchtime, there were fruits, soups, and meats. "The food smelled so nice" that Joseph was always first in line for it. There were even covers for the prisoners' beds and sheets were changed once a week. What really got to his Soviet trained eyes, however, was the gymnasium where prisoners could exercise every day of the week. He marveled that, especially with regular use of weight-lifts, a prisoner could actually leave the jail physically stronger than when he entered, and he wondered whether or not this bade well for society.

Several weeks after his arrival, Joseph acquired yet another icon of ism: a Ford, though it was old and badly beaten up, but better than the Lada back in Minsk. Alex first faced the trials and ordeals of getting a driver's license. He failed the test two times in a row, and then Uncle Vladimir gave him some practical advice.

"Alex, you know what you have to do to pass this test. Get an envelope and put $30.00 in it. Then leave it on the driver's seat when you get out, while the instructor is adding up your points. Just leave it, just like you have forgotten to take it with you."

On his third attempt, the officer said to Alex, "You have prepared very well. Certainly, you pass the test. (A few years later such activities became the focus of investigations, as it was found that the crush of Soviet and Latino immigrants caused money to take the place of verbal communications).

And so the Gavi family was introduced to yet another aspect of Capitalism: "Money Talks!"

A few weeks later, Joseph had no problem getting his own driver's license.

Each morning the jail's "big door" opened just long enough for the employees to enter. If you arrived later than 6:50 a.m., you were locked out, and would lose a day's pay.

JOSEPH On the way to work one day, I am late, and know if I miss the 6:50 deadline, I will be out of luck. I ran a red-light, and was spotted by one of Chicago's finest.

I just keep driving, looking straight ahead, ignoring all the flashing lights. The officer drove right up beside me and turned on his siren. Even then it took a while for me to appear that I just suddenly noticed him. I pulled over to the curb.

The policeman was a bit angry. "You ran a red-light," he said to me, "and you would not stop."

I explained my situation: I had to be at the jail by 6:50; otherwise, I would lose a day's pay.

The officer told me, "Okay, either you pay $35.00 now, or you have to go to the court over this matter, and have your license suspended."

I did not quite understand what the officer was telling me. I do know that I did not have the $35.00 on me. Who in their right mind would travel around Chicago with that much cash in their pocket?

I accept a court appearance – my driver's license suspended except for getting to and from work – for 24 December 1979. I got to work on time, but just barely. I told my workers about the ordeal with the traffic cop. They all started to laugh.

"Look," a friend told me. "It's still two months before you have to appear in court on this matter. Just tell the judge that you were in the middle of the intersection when the light turned red. Nobody's going to convict you of a minor traffic offense on Christmas Eve."

Sure enough, when I appear in court, I told the judge what I had been instructed to do. The officer was present, but said he couldn't remember the details. The judge ordered my case dismissed and my license fully restored. It was a fine holiday season for all us Gavis.

After a year or so in Chicago, the Gavi family was prospering. Ida worked in a barber shop as a manicurist. She had begun to feel comfortable in America when, as she walked down a street one morning, a citizen smiled at her and said, "hi." She said "hi" to the next person she met, who smiled and answered "hello" back to her. "In Russia you are supposed just to keep your mouth shut, but in America we had this wonderful freedom of speech." Zina found work in a large department store, and Isaac continued to work as an engineer for a large construction company. "We felt very safe," Joseph and Ida say, especially because their nuclear family was still together as a unit. Family unity was the first and most significant thing for the Gavis – even greater than immigrating to America. If they had had to split the family to come to America, they probably would not have done it.

But as the economic depression deepened in 1980, Joseph, along with two hundred of his fellow workers, was laid off from the Cook County Jail. He qualified for unemployment benefits of $780.00 a month, so the family was not in totally dire straits.

Nevertheless, they all considered that their jobs were in dead-end areas; there was no upward mobility. Their friends, the family Zlatin, had immigrated directly to Louisville, Kentucky, and the two families from time to time exchanged visits. Joseph liked Louisville because, among other things, it was easy – at least compared to Chicago – to get to the countryside. One did not have to drive "hours and hours," or so it seemed, through suburbs, to get to the rural areas. Also, it was about the same size of Minsk.

Louisville offered the Gavis what they and a real estate company with an international program, considered a life-long career: operating a restaurant, thereby becoming small business owners.

JOSEPH Only five or six times in my entire life have I even eaten in a restaurant except in the navy, and now it seems all of a sudden I own one!

Ida did not particularly want to operate a restaurant: "I knew nothing about it." Besides, since she knew how to type in the Russian language, she wished to get some translation work, and to learn to type in English, and work in an office. But she bowed to the inevitable.

They moved to Louisville in 1981, rented an apartment, and acquired a little restaurant on South Seventh Street. It was primarily a take-out restaurant, and for the Gavis, it was a disaster.

JOSEPH We had to answer the telephone to make deliveries, and we could not understand what the customers were ordering. On our first day of business, we grossed $375.00. In three days it was down to $55.00. Obviously, some kind of linguistic help was in order here. Our real estate agent's two sons came over and voluntarily took orders for several hours a day, and this helped some, but it was far from a permanent solution.

Isaac had remained in Chicago, working for the Harza Construction Company, a firm that employed over 1,000 engineers. When his current project ended, the company wanted to transfer him to West Virginia, but he figured that his family in Louisville needed him. For one thing, he had a facility with English that neither Joseph nor Ida nor even Alex possessed. By now he and Zina had another child, besides David; so the four of them moved to Kentucky. And, Isaac's English began to turn the restaurant's fortunes around.

On the happy occasion of taking up residence in the Bluegrass State, Isaac and his family did not immediately move in with Joseph and Ida – as they had always done before – they got their own apartment. And this arrangement was not only unsatisfactory because they wanted to keep the family together as much as possible (though Alex did go back to Chicago), it was also un-acceptably expensive. Between the two families – Joseph's and Isaac's – the monthly rent for their apartments was perilously close to the thousand dollar mark. And Joseph's (and Isaac's, too, for he also was a graduate of the Minsk Polytechnic Institute) practical mind, imbued by years of experience in the Soviet Union, told him that this figure was ludicrous.

Why not, then, acquire a house of their own, for all the family. All the houses they looked at were beyond their financial reach. But they found a lot they could afford, and since Isaac was a civil engineer, the family thought: why not build our own residence? They went to St. Helen's bank and borrowed $45,000 "from the nice people there."

JOSEPH   Our first plan was to hire a contractor (at a fee of $250.00 a day), and have our home built to our specifications. It did not take us long to spot the contractor's machinations and slow-downs. Two or three days in a row, he just pushed the time. He didn't do anything, so I exercised another tool of the Capitalism I was learning: I fired him.

The main structure of the house was finished, and Isaac and I began to roam around Louisville where houses were being built, to determine how they were finished. We were truthful with all the builders we met. We want to do our own house ourselves, I always told them. The Louisville builders were good-natured, and I guess somewhat bemused with our strange accents, and told us to watch as much as we wanted to, and even offered practical advice. I marveled at this cooperation: would I have had the same experience in Chicago? I knew beyond a doubt that I would not in Minsk.

Isaac visited all the Sears-Roebuck stores in the area to see what tools were necessary for indoor trimming and finishing. As a result of all this "watching," Isaac and Joseph put in their own mahogany walls and did all the living room floor work and bathroom tiles. At the outset, they hoped for a house of some 2,000 square feet, but when they dug out a basement and then added a large apartment over their ground-level garage, they realized that their total living space was going to be close to 5,000 square feet. "We had never had this kind of room before. So much space! So much space, we have!" It was overwhelming to these two Soviet families who had never experienced so much as a third of all that room.

JOSEPH   Well, if we Gavis could do all of this for ourselves, why couldn't we do it for other people? After all, this was the land of Capitalism, where entrepreneurial exertions were welcome all the way from Washington to local Chambers of Commerce. Thus was born the Gavi Construction Company, run mostly by Isaac, but with enough contributions from me that it did become a family affair. After fewer than four years in the United States we were living the American Dream. We were quickly losing our status as Comrade and becoming Citizen.

And we built a house, and sold it for a profit. And then we built another house and also gained a profit. I like this! I exclaimed.

Nevertheless, it was a slow process. While running the restaurant, they could finish only two or three houses a year: they could not depend on construction for their entire income. Isaac worked all day with Gavi Homebuilders, while Joseph and the rest of the family coped with the restaurant. It was stressful, but exciting.

Gavi Homebuilders ultimately became so successful that the company won Louisville's prestigious "Homerama" award from the city's home building association. But then, another Capitalist reality set in. Their clients were not always up front with them. Some were either late or very late, or they could not pay at all. It was time consuming and expensive to take them to court.

Then yet one more Capitalist problem occurred for the Gavi family: stomach problems, or ulcers. Isaac finally decided that he needed a rest from it all. He found a job with the City of Louisville as a code enforcer, a position he still holds as the Twentieth Century comes to a close.

Joseph and Ida's younger son, Alex, wanted to be a musician. When he was in high school, Joseph constantly admonished Alex to get a solid education, so that he would make a good living for himself and his future family. "Ah, Papa," he kept telling Joseph, "I have plenty of time."

And, of course, it did not take Joseph long to give a Capitalist response to such assertions. "There is one thing, young Alex, that you cannot buy, and that is time." Ultimately, at the University of Illinois, Alex became a computer programmer, and afterward was hired by the United States Federal Reserve Bank. Today, he works at the Echlan Automotive Systems in Chicago as their computer specialist.

Back at the restaurant, the cooks came and went, but with each one the

Gavis learned a bit more English – one or two words a day. And so slowly, slowly, they became inured to American ways.

Above Gavi's Restaurant in the Legal Arts Building was Kentucky's division of the Internal Revenue Service, and the Gavi family became friendly with the federal tax collectors. One day Joseph was talking with an IRS lady about his troubles with the restaurant – not just the language but, apparently, the quality of food as well – and she said, "Joseph, you need to find the guy who ran the restaurant before you came to town. His name is Sam Bird."

JOSEPH   To be sure I start asking questions about Sam Bird. After several days a woman walks in and asks if I need a grill cook.

"Well, yes, of course, do I ever!" was my response to her.

"I am asking for my husband," the woman said. "He worked here before for ten years. Right now he is unemployed. Maybe you could give him his old job back."

Maybe, I answered. "What is his name?"

"Sam Bird."

Yes, indeed, I hired Sam Bird who became a part of our family. He is still with us even today. He is the center of everything, a good organizer. He knows exactly what to do.

But for Joseph and Ida and the other family members, to be hiring someone to work for them – another major Capitalistic practice – was worlds apart from the subservient positions they had always held in the Soviet Union. Heady stuff, this, being Capitalist – but more important – a Citizen. His Capitalism was conditioned by humaneness, by the memory that he had spent almost the first fifty years of his life under a Communist regime which, he sometimes recalled, betrayed him.

One day in 1985, Ida and Joseph closed the restaurant at noon and headed for Louisville's federal building. There, in the early afternoon, they joined a dozen other people, and confirmed the naturalization papers and petitions for citizenship which earlier they had taken out.

"There was no emotion," Ida recalls, "except that we were touched that our neighbor, attorney Steve Early, whom we had known for only a short time, came to witness our becoming American citizens. We have never forgotten that act of kindness."

JOSEPH   Right across the alleyway from our restaurant and opening out onto South Seventh Street, was Mazzoni's Oyster Bar. It was getting ready to go out of business, why I don't know. We feared that someone serving food similar to us [hamburgers – mostly American food, but their popular vegetable soup is widely acclaimed as "pure Russian," and their roast chicken always gets into the big newspaper food columns] might move in and offer us some unwanted competition (there's Capitalism again!), so we took advantage of the good deal offered us.

At least at the beginning of their restaurant experience, the Gavis offered take-out. Joseph himself used to deliver lunches to offices around town. Little did his take-out patrons realize that this diminutive man standing in front of them with the strange accent, was a Doctor of Physiology, mountain climber extraordinaire, multi-linguist, and survivor of the holocaust.

And when Joseph did not deliver lunches, Isaac, a trained engineer, did. "It doesn't harm my intelligence to do that," he claims. "I meet people from every walk of life from all levels. I learn by doing it.[37] His mother and father, Isaac said, are proud because "they own" the restaurant. "It's theirs. They're making it work. And no one asks any questions about their business in the dead of night."[38] It is the opportunity in this country that the Family Gavi cherishes the most; "anybody," they say, "can work here if they really want to."

Though they serve only breakfast and lunch, Joseph and Ida have opened at night for special occasions. One such was when Spanish exchange students visited Doss High School in Louisville. Joseph believed early on that it is his civic duty to accept invitations from schools and clubs who want him to talk about the holocaust and expound on life in the Soviet Union.

For examples, he addressed Louisville's branch of B'Nai B'rith in 1985. It director wrote to Joseph afterward: "Your experiences during the holocaust were most unforgettable and your personal accounting was very moving…. Your story made a lasting impression on all who attended."[39]

Two months later he spoke to Junior Achievement about the differences between a controlled economy in the Soviet Union and a relatively

[37] Tom Van Howe,"The Gavi Family Finds Freedom…."

[38] Ibid.

[39] Sue Goodman, letter to Joseph Gavi, 23 April 1985. Gavi Collection, Louisville, Kentucky.

free one in the United States. Additionally, he has given speeches several times at the University of Louisville.

Since 1989 the Gavi family has operated the restaurant fronting onto Seventh Street, just across from the police station. Many lawyers, judges, policemen (of whom Joseph is no longer afraid), and plain, ordinary citizens have long patronized Gavi's Restaurant. Why? Not just for the roast chicken. They can "hear" America while having lunch. Joseph good-naturedly "patrols" the premises, engaging conversations on every subject under the sun, ranging from the latest scandal in Washington to the status of education in Kentucky.

In his restaurant today, Joseph talks with anybody and everybody who has even the slightest something to say. He is making up for all those years in the Soviet Union when he had to watch his tongue. He knows that in Louisville, people can and do disagree with him, but he does not fear the midnight knock on the door for expressing his own opinions.

Joseph Gavi and his entire family relish the thought of waking up each morning and engaging in dialogue with friends and neighbors, restaurant patrons, or for that matter, rank strangers, and being protected by the First Amendment to the United States Constitution. Free speech was something the Gavis – and thousands of their Soviet countrymen as well – dreamed about while in the Old Country, but dared not practice.

Joseph Gavi has reached a reflective time in his life. Who, in their wildest imaginations back in 1941, when he "faced" the axman in his dreams, would have contemplated that he would become a well-known restaurateur in a large Southern city of the United States?

Who could have thought of any redemption when he struggled to get loved ones and others out of the Minsk ghetto, sometimes right in front of hateful German guards? Or when he served the Russian partisans, or the Soviet navy? Or when he was stranded on a narrow ledge on Mount Bashkara and thought he and all his comrades were going to die?

Life is full of wonders, Joseph Gavi and his family know, and today they try to pass on that premise – and indeed that promise – to people they meet. Whatever makes you down and out today can surely be changed by tomorrow. They are living examples of hope; and success, security, and happiness, the end result of that hope.

A NOTE ON SOURCES

T he overwhelming material for this book came from Joseph Gavi. I interviewed him some thirty-five to forty hours. Also I got materials and interviews from Ida, Joseph's wife, and from their son, Alex. To corroborate and clarify the experiences in the Minsk ghetto, the following secondary sources were most useful to me: Hersh Smoliar, The Minsk Ghetto. trans. by Hyman J. Lewbin, 1966; Shalom Cholavsky, "The German Jews in the Minsk Ghetto," in Yad Vashem Studies, No. 17, 1986, pp. 219-249; Reuben Ainsztein, Jewish Resistance in Nazi-Occupied Eastern Europe; "Eliyahu Mushkin," in Encyclopedia of the Holocaust, Vol. 3, 1990; Encyclopedia of Judica, Vol. 12, p. 56; "Minsk," in Encyclopedia of Judaica, Vol.12, pp. 51-58; and Gerald Reitlinger, The Final Solution: The Attempt to Exterminate the Jews of Europe, 1939-1945, 1953. The Moscow Times interview of Anna Krasnoperko about conditions in the Minsk ghetto was informative as well.

Joseph Gavi smuggled his academic works out of the Soviet Union, including his prized Ph.D dissertation. They are in his private collections in his home in Louisville, Kentucky. I collected about a dozen of the twenty-nine scientific articles that Joseph Gavi wrote or co-authored. Professor Hugh Phillips, the Soviet specialist at Western Kentucky University's History Department, read enough of each of these articles for me to know their titles, their specific subject, and the names of the journals in which they were published.

The New York Times for 1977 and 1978 was most useful for documenting the numbers of Soviet citizens applying for permission to leave the Soviet Union and go to Israel or, as with the Gavis, the United States. Howard Sachar's Diaspora: An Inquiry Into the Contemporary World, 1985, was enlightening as well.

For the Gavi's sojourn in Louisville, I used articles in local newspapers, and letters written to the Gavis from various members of the community. These are all housed in the Gavi Collection.

INDEX

– A –

Abalakov, Vitaly 104
Abrasha (Aunt Liza's husband) 90
Adil-Su 105
Afghanistan 126, 127, 128, 129, 130, 134, 149
Agronovski, Gera 105, 106, 112, 113, 114
Ainsztein, Reuben 32, 196
Alber, Solomon 168
Albert, Yakov 168
Alek (Joseph's friend) 48
Alla (Ida's sister) 159, 181, 184
Amer (family dog) 174, 175, 176, 177, 178, 181, 184
American (America) 5, 13, 14, 20, 29, 157, 164, 165, 167, 169,
    171, 173, 175, 177, 179, 180, 181, 182, 183, 185,
    186, 187, 189, 191, 192, 193, 194, 195
Andreev, Andrey Andreevich 107
Andreev, Volodia 107
anti-Semitic 20, 26, 39, 40, 45, 86, 136, 168
Armstrong, Dave (Mayor) 14, 15
Arutunian, Ruben 175
Aunt Fanya 28
Aunt Liza 27, 28, 88, 89, 90, 95
Aunt Manya 28, 34
Aunt Polia 28
Austria/Austrian/Austrians 26, 39, 40, 174, 176, 177

– B –

Baksam 105
Baltic Navy School 91
Baranovichi 64, 74, 75, 78, 80
Bashkara (mountain) 114, 115, 116, 120, 121, 195
Belarus 4, 13, 17, 25, 33, 66, 67
Belsky, A. (Partisan commander) 56
Berlin 39
Bird, Sam 16, 151, 193
Bisenga 105
Black Sea 103
Bluegrass State 190
B'Nai B'rith 194
Boruchovich, Lenia 120, 121, 122
Bosnia 10
Bowling Green 8, 11, 15
Brailovsky, Viktor 168
Bremen 39
Brest 28, 30, 172, 175
Bulegin, Professor 153
Burba, Paula 14
Byelorussia/Byelorussian(s) 19, 25, 26, 29, 31, 34, 35, 36, 37,
    38, 41, 46, 47, 49, 50, 54, 59, 62, 63, 74, 84, 101,
    103, 109, 110, 125, 153, 155, 156, 179, 186
Byelorussian Polytechnic Institute 17, 110, 125, 153, 158, 159,
    164, 191
Byelorussian Technical Institute 156

– C –

Canada 177
Capitalism/Capitalist(s) 20, 26, 27, 184, 185, 188, 191, 192,
    193, 194
Carter, Jimmy (U.S. President) 168
Caspian Sea 103
Caucasus (Mountains) 12, 17, 102, 103, 114, 121, 139, 140, 147
Chicago 9, 12, 159, 178, 181, 183, 185, 186, 188, 189, 190,
    191, 192
China 126, 128, 129, 143, 168
Cholavsky, Shalom 32, 39, 196
Chvalensk 29
Communism/Communist(s) 8, 17, 19, 27, 29, 30, 31, 34, 42,
    51, 84, 85, 87, 162, 163, 180, 193
Cook County Jail 187, 189

Crestwood 10, 14
Czechoslovakia 39, 60, 175, 176
Czechs 40

– D –

Davis, Lloyd and Sam 15
Delmonico's 185
Djan-Tugan Plateau (mountain) 114, 119, 120, 121
Dombai 105
Drozdy Plaza 31
Dusseldorf 39

– E –

Echlan Automotive Systems 192
Engels, Sima (Ida's mother) 159, 160
English 13, 16, 18, 181, 186, 187, 190, 193
Europe 10, 32, 39, 67, 92, 103, 143, 186, 196

– F –

Fania (Ida's sister) 159, 165
Federal Reserve Bank 192
Fedia (Isaac's friend) 160
Fera (Joseph's cousin)
Filimonov, Leo 112
Fima (cousin) 89
Flaksa Street 57, 58, 60
Formicino Flea Market 181
Frankfurt 39
F. Skorini Street 148

– G –

Gabriel (Gaba) (Joseph's grandson) 10, 12, 14
Gacy, John Wayne 187
Gaiche (village) 53, 54, 58
Gaichi 53
Gavi, Alex (Joseph's son) 11, 12, 13, 14, 123, 125, 126, 138,
    139, 150, 165, 166, 167, 169, 170, 171, 173, 174,
    175, 178, 180, 184, 185, 186, 188, 190, 192, 196
Gavi Construction Company 192
Gavi, David (Isaac's son) 9, 10, 15, 16, 28, 32, 50, 54, 182, 184,
    186, 190
Gavi Homebuilders 192
Gavi, Ida (nee Engels) 4, 12, 13, 16, 18, 20, 29, 67, 109, 110,
    111, 112, 123, 124, 125, 126, 127, 128, 129, 130,
    131, 132, 133, 134, 135, 136, 138, 139, 142, 147,
    149, 150, 156, 158, 159, 160, 161, 162, 164, 165,
    167, 169, 170, 173, 174, 175, 177, 178, 179, 180,
    181, 182, 183, 184, 189, 190, 192, 193, 194, 196
Gavi, Isaac (Joseph's son) 12, 110, 111, 112, 123, 125, 126, 132,
    138, 139, 152, 159, 160, 165, 167, 169, 170, 173,
    174, 175, 178, 180, 181, 182, 184, 186, 189, 190,
    191, 192, 194
Gavi, Isaac (Joseph's uncle) 27, 28, 31, 67
Gavi, Leva (Joseph's brother) 28, 30, 37, 38, 40, 41, 42, 46, 47,
    49, 50, 52, 57, 60, 62, 63, 64, 78, 82, 83, 84, 93, 97,
    102, 169, 185
Gavi, Natalie 14
Gavi, Naum (Joseph's father) 27, 28, 29, 30, 31, 37, 39, 47, 48,
    49, 53, 168
Gavi, Rachel (Joseph's mother) 26, 27, 28, 29, 30, 40, 51, 52, 53,
    54, 61, 82, 83, 84, 89, 93, 95, 96, 97, 100, 110, 123,
    125, 126, 169
Gavi, Shaya (Joseph's paternal grandfather) 27, 28, 30, 34, 43, 47
Gavi's Restaurant 9, 13, 16, 18, 151, 193, 195
Gavi, Zina (Isaac's wife) 16, 167, 169, 170, 173, 174, 175, 178,
    179, 180, 181, 182, 184, 189, 190
Gendarme (mountain) 120
German(s)/Germany 11, 15, 19, 26, 28, 29, 30, 31, 32, 33, 34,

35, 36, 37, 38, 39, 40, 41, 42, 43, 44, 45, 46, 48, 49,
  50, 51, 52, 53, 54, 55, 56, 57, 60, 61, 62, 64, 67, 68,
  70, 73, 74, 75, 76, 76, 77, 78, 89, 92, 103, 110, 161,
  174, 187, 195, 196
Gestapo 48, 50, 53
Ghiang Shan (border of China) 143
Gimpel, Tonichka 54
Goethe 39
Gogol Library 181
Golfand, Yuri 168
Gomel 29, 84, 85, 87, 153
Goodman, Sue 194
Gorkin 87, 88
Greendwig, Alter 158, 159
Greendwig, Evsey 159
Greendwig, Lisa 159
Greendwig, Morris 159
Greendwig, Silvia 159
Greendwig, Sima 12, 54, 159, 160, 178
Grushevski-Poselok 28, 30, 31, 40, 83
Gulf of Finland 92
gypsy 42

– H –

Haman the Amalekite 46
Hamburg 39
Hammer, Bunya 54
Harrison, Lowell 8
Harrison, Lowell H. 20
Harza Construction Company 190
Hebrew Immigration Aid Society (HIAS) 173, 177, 178, 179,
  180, 181, 182, 183, 184, 185
Hindu Kush 126
Holocaust 4, 5, 9, 10, 14, 35, 42, 43, 45, 47, 49, 51, 196

– I –

Internal Revenue Service 193
Isia 28, 47
Israel 56, 160, 162, 167, 168, 169, 170, 173, 176, 177, 179, 197

– J –

Jenia (Ida's niece) 159
Jew(s)/Jewish 4, 10, 15, 19, 20, 26, 27, 31, 32, 33, 34, 35, 36, 37,
  38, 39, 40, 41, 42, 45, 46, 47, 48, 49, 50, 51, 53, 54,
  56, 57, 58, 59, 66, 67, 68, 77, 86, 92, 110, 131, 136,
  154, 156, 157, 159, 160, 162, 163, 164, 167, 168,
  170, 176, 179, 186, 196
Johnson, Jim 15
Judenrat 35, 46, 51

– K –

Kalinin, Michael (Speaker of the Russian Parliment) 87
Kant, Immanuel 39
Karakorum 126
Katuzov Detachment 56
Katyn Forests 77
Kazinets, Isai Pavlovich 35
Kentucky 7, 8, 9, 11, 12, 13, 15, 16, 17, 19, 20, 124, 151, 155,
  174, 179, 189, 190, 193, 194, 195, 196
KGB (Secret Police) 49, 123, 126, 128, 175
Khergiani, Misha 119, 120, 121, 124
Khlebanov 53, 55
Khlebanov, Tzilia 53
Kiev 85, 86, 87, 89, 153, 166, 167
Klenskiy, David 54
Koffmann, Greta 51, 52, 53, 118
Komsomol (Communist Youth) 87
Kosovo 10
Krasnoperko, Anna 45, 196
Kube, Wilhelm (Commisar) 35, 36, 39
Kulvanovsky, Mecheslav (Professor) 153, 154, 155
Kunlun 126
Kutuzov (Partisan group) 55, 78

Kzel, Vladimir 104

– L –

Lada (automobile) 161, 166, 167, 173, 184, 188
LaGrange 9, 10
Lapidus, Israel (Partisan commander) 56
Lenin 65, 71, 120, 149
Leningrad 27, 88, 89, 90, 91, 92, 93, 95, 153, 173
Lenin Square 65
Leonov, Ivan 104
Lerner, Aleksandr 168
Lewbin, Hyman J. 32, 196
Liberation Day 56
Livchitz, Chaim 152
Louisville (Kentucky) 7, 8, 9, 10, 12, 13, 14, 15, 17, 18, 19, 124,
  132, 151, 174, 179, 189, 190, 191, 192, 193, 194,
  195, 196, 197

– M –

Malena(s) 37, 40, 47, 49
Maly Trostinetz 38, 39
Mama (Rachel Gavi) 26, 28, 29, 34, 37, 38, 40, 41, 42, 46, 47,
  49, 50, 51, 52, 54, 57, 60, 62, 63, 83, 84, 87, 94, 96,
  101, 102, 103, 118
Marshrut 114
Mazzoni's Oyster Bar 194
Medvezhino (village) 53, 62
Michener, James A. 129
Minsk (capital of Byelorussia: Today, Belarus) 4, 5, 7, 9, 12, 15,
  17, 18, 19, 25, 26, 27, 28, 29, 30, 31, 32, 33, 34, 35,
  36, 37, 38, 39, 40, 41, 42, 47, 48, 49, 51, 53, 54, 57,
  58, 60, 62, 65, 66, 67, 69, 70, 71, 77, 82, 83, 84, 85,
  87, 88, 89, 90, 91, 92, 93, 94, 95, 97, 98, 99, 101,
  104, 107, 109, 110, 111, 121, 123, 124, 125, 126,
  136, 146, 148, 150, 152, 155, 157, 158, 159, 160,
  161, 162, 164, 165, 166, 167, 169, 171, 173, 174,
  175, 177, 178, 179, 183, 185, 186, 187, 188, 190,
  191, 195, 196
Mogilev Road 45
Molotov, Vyacheslav 30
Moscow 31, 41, 45, 47, 54, 57, 60, 64, 75, 82, 84, 85, 86, 87,
  88, 90, 107, 110, 138, 153, 155, 168, 185, 196
Mount Elbrus 67, 103, 143
Mushkin, Eliyahu 35, 36, 196

– N –

Nacra-Tau (mountain) 106
Naleboki Forest 53, 55, 56, 77, 78, 80, 82
Natasha (cousin) 89
Nazi 10, 30, 32, 35, 38, 39, 50, 54, 55, 56, 57, 61, 64, 84, 124,
  196
Nazis 10, 11, 17, 29, 30, 35, 36, 37, 38, 47, 50, 53, 57, 76, 109
Negoreloe 76
Nemiga Street 32, 70
New York 10, 32, 35, 39, 159, 168, 183, 197
Nichiporovich (Professor) 110
NKVD (secret police) 27

– O –

Obuwnaya Street 33
Ontogenesis 155
Orenienbaum (port) 90, 93, 94, 95
Ostia 180, 182, 183, 185
Ostrovskaya Street 33
Ostrovsky Street 38

– P –

Pakistan 126, 129
Palestine Liberation Organization (PLO) 176, 179
Paley, Hannah (Joseph's maternal grandmother) 27, 28, 46, 47
Paley, Kiva (Joseph's maternal grandfather) 26, 27, 28, 30, 43, 46,
  47, 49, 50, 51, 60, 63

Pamirs (mountains) 126, 127, 132, 133, 142, 148, 169
Pan American Airlines 180, 182, 183
Papa (Naum Gavi) 26, 28, 29, 33, 37, 38, 40, 41, 42, 44, 45, 46,
    47, 48, 49, 54, 83, 192
Partisan(s) 5, 17, 18, 19, 33, 35, 36, 43, 44, 45, 47, 48, 53, 54,
    55, 56, 57, 58, 59, 60, 61, 62, 63, 64, 72, 73, 74, 75,
    76, 77, 78, 79, 80, 81, 82, 84, 85, 86, 94, 96, 108,
    109, 121, 123, 145, 147, 155, 174, 195
Patton, Paul (Governor of Kentucky) 9
Peterson, Sima 54
Phillips, Hugh 20, 155, 196
Pinsk 29
Poland/Poles/Polish 19, 26, 29, 30, 33, 39, 54, 77, 78, 79, 82,
    175, 176, 187
POWs 44

– R –

Reitlinger, Gerald 39, 196
Respublikanskaya Street 33, 40
Rome 175, 177, 179, 180, 181, 182, 183, 185
Romulo, Carlos 17
Rubek, Arutunaian 150
Rubenina, Valya 54
Russia/Russian 17, 18, 19, 26, 27, 30, 32, 34, 35, 36, 54, 56,
    58, 73, 74, 76, 77, 78, 79, 82, 83, 87, 89, 92, 100,
    108, 110, 114, 128, 129, 130, 134, 149, 158, 159,
    160, 161, 172, 173, 176, 181, 183, 185, 187, 189,
    190, 194, 195
Rwanda 10

– S –

Sachar, Howard M. 168
Sacks, Jonathan 15
Samarkand 127, 128, 129, 130, 135
Sarah 28, 47
Schelda 105
Sears-Roebuck 191
Seava (Ida's nephew) 159
Shatsk (village) 158, 159
Sherokay Street 33
Shirokaya Street 31, 32
Shurowski (peak) 140
Slavery Square 32
Slepak, Vladimir and Mariya 168
Smilovichi 26, 27
Smoliar, Hersh 32, 196
South Seventh Street 16, 190, 194
Sovetskaya 65, 71, 148
Sovetskaya Street 65, 148
Soviet 9, 13, 17, 18, 19, 20, 25, 26, 29, 30, 32, 42, 49, 59, 60,
    64, 67, 75, 77, 78, 84, 85, 86, 90, 91, 92, 94, 95, 97,
    98, 101, 103, 104, 105, 107, 108, 111, 112, 114, 119,
    121, 123, 124, 125, 126, 127, 128, 131, 136, 145,
    153, 154, 155, 157, 159, 160, 162, 163, 165, 166,
    167, 168, 169, 170, 171, 172, 173, 174, 175, 177,
    179, 183, 184, 185, 187, 188, 191, 193, 194, 195,
    196, 197
Soviet Army 19, 170
Soviet Navy 17, 19, 67, 92, 95, 108, 131, 195
Soviet Union (Soviet Socialist Republics) 9, 13, 18, 19, 20, 26,
    29, 32, 49, 60, 85, 86, 91, 98, 111, 112, 121, 123,
    125, 127, 153, 155, 160, 163, 165, 166, 167, 168,
    169, 170, 172, 173, 174, 175, 183, 184, 185, 187,
    191, 193, 194, 195, 196, 197

SS (German political police) 30, 31, 38, 39, 51, 59
Stalin, Josef 8, 77, 78, 98
Staroe Selo (village) 53, 54, 55, 57, 58, 59, 60, 61, 62, 63
Star of David 50
Suchaya Street 33, 49, 57
Sukenek 37
Suvorov Military Academy 84

– T –

Tajikistan 126
Tamberlane 127
Tashkent 126, 127, 132, 179
Tel Aviv 177
Tian Shan 126
Tzilia 53, 54, 55, 56, 57

– U –

Ubileynaya Plaza 32, 35, 38, 39, 48, 49
Ukraine 33, 166
Ulu-Tau-Chana 113
Uncle Abrasha 89, 90
Uncle David 28, 32
Uncle Isaac 27, 28
Uncle Sholem 27
United States/US/USA 4, 7, 9, 11, 12, 13, 19, 20, 110, 150,
    160, 162, 167, 168, 170, 171, 173, 175, 176, 177,
    178, 179, 183, 185, 192, 195, 197
University of Illinois 192
USSR 12, 19, 103, 104, 114, 136, 155, 162, 167, 168

– V –

Valery (Ida's brother-in-law) 159, 178, 181, 184
Van Howe, Tom 194
Vienna 39, 172, 174, 176, 177, 178, 179, 180, 183, 184, 185
Vishnevski 56
Vitebsk 29
Vladimir (Ida's brother) 104, 168, 184, 187, 188
Volga River 29
Volkovisk (Poland) 79
Volkov, Yuri 126
Voroshilov Machine Factory/Tank Repair Factory 36, 42, 46, 53
Vyazma 41

– W –

Washington, DC 192, 195
Western Kentucky University 8, 20, 155, 196

– Y –

Yakubovski, Ivan Vasilievich (Captain of the Red Army) 78, 79,
    82, 83, 84
Yugoslavia 60

– Z –

Zamkovaya Street 48
Zhukov Brigade/Division 72, 78, 145, 147
Zlatin (family) 189
Zomer, Tonya 54
Zoring, Shlomo 56, 63, 78, 82
Zubkov, V. 112, 113